# THE HOLY GOOF

## A Biography of NEAL CASSADY

*by William Plummer*

**PARAGON HOUSE**
NEW YORK

*For Molly*

First Paperback edition, 1990

Published in the United States by
Paragon House
90 Fifth Avenue
New York, NY 10011

Library of Congress Cataloging-in-Publication Data

Plummer, William, 1945–
The holy goof : a biography of Neal Cassady / by
William Plummer. — 1st paperback ed.
p.     cm.
Reprint. Originally published: Englewood Cliffs, N.J. :
Prentice-Hall, c1981.
ISBN 1-55778-287-3
1. Cassady, Neal.   2. Kerouac, Jack, 1922–1969—
Friends and associates.   3. Beat generation—Biography.
4. United States—Biography.   I. Title.
[CT275.C3458P59   1990]
973.92′092—dc20
[B]     89-22818     CIP

Manufactured in the United States of America

10 9 8 7 6 5 4 3 2 1

# CONTENTS

PART ONE

THE
BARBER'S
BOY

*America when will you be angelic?*
*When will you take off your clothes?*

from ALLEN GINSBERG's *"America"*

Jack Kerouac had to wait six years, until September 1957, to see *On the Road* published. Rejection embittered him and, perhaps, shrank his soul. But had Kerouac been requited by the publishing industry in 1951, he probably would not have plunged so furiously into his work and produced, among other titles, the involuted *Visions of Cody*, the phantasmagoric *Doctor Sax*, the heart's cry that is *Tristessa*. Conceived with little hope of publication, these "difficult" books were contoured and charged by failure. Still more important, for the purposes of history: Had *On the Road* been released in 1951, the chances are it would have been passed over by reviewers and public alike as a curiosity. The nation was not yet ready for a programmatically raw book written in "bop prosody" and chronicling endless cross-country trips by a pair of—depending upon how one looks at them— "holy barbarians" or "giggling nihilists." Kerouac's book was an inadvertent manifesto awaiting its moment.

That that moment was just beginning to build in 1951 can be seen from any of several vantages. It can be seen, above all, in the striking change in the fare at the American movie house, in the decline of the rosy-cheeked

lyric sensibility of the MGM musical, and in the rise of
the coolly seething archetype of Marlon Brando and
James Dean:

1951 *An American in Paris*
1952 *Singin' in the Rain*
1953 *The Wild One*
*The Band Wagon*
1954 *On the Waterfront*
1955 *It's Always Fair Weather*
*Guys and Dolls*
*East of Eden*
*Rebel Without a Cause**

Massive discontent was gathering in 1951. A "shit-storm"
was in the offing.

When its time came, *On the Road* could not have
had a more dramatic announcement. Within weeks of its
debut the Russians sent up the world's first manmade
satellite. Although the State Department initially tried to
dismiss Sputnik as the Soviets' little "bauble," the satellite
clearly chilled the country. It was apparent as well that
the launching of Sputnik and the advent of the Beat
Generation twinned in the public mind and triggered
much the same dis-ease. For almost instantly the Beats
were known by the nervous, if snide, diminutive,
"beatnik."

Although *On the Road* crept onto the best-seller
list for a spell, it was more notably a *succès de scandale.*

---

*This graphic taken from Michael Wood's *America in the Movies* (1975).

A line was drawn; sides picked themselves. Fence-sitting was out of the question. Sadly, literary merit, for most people—excepting of course the avant-garde, the Black Mountain College crowd, which was electrified by Kerouac's achievement—was beside the point. For both fans and detractors alike, Kerouac's instant classic mostly served to herald the arrival in coastal centers of legions of young men and women intent upon kicks—would-be "hipsters" out to raise the ante of sensation by way of drugs, jazz, sex, petty criminality, by way of any attitude or activity that might be parlayed into a rush of exhiliration, into proof that they were pulsatingly alive.

These were not the Fabulous Fifties of our revisionist nostalgia but, in Robert Lowell's phrase, the "tranquilized fifties." Suffice to say, as many have, that the postwar years constituted an Age of Consensus: the consensus being that the American way of life was unimpeachable and that it was menaced by communism, the cultural consequence being a bland amalgam of complacency and deep-seated fear. Yet the burning issue for the young and disaffected, who had little memory of the War and less of the Depression, was not the Russians and bourgeois well-being. Rather it was the atrophy of the Self. "We now live in a universe where there is no echo of 'I'" ventured one contemporary thinker. *On the Road* seemed to offer an alternative to "growing up absurd," to being "upwardly mobile" in "the lonely crowd." It seemed to offer a higher-octane mode of being.

Kerouac became a *cause célèbre*. Old-guard radicals faulted his rebellion for being apolitical, asocial, and amoral. Time/Life, representing the Establishment with a curious vengeance, blamed Kerouac for the weekend bohemians with their Do-It-Yourself Beatnik Kits; for the cooled-out, bearded, bathless cats, who with their chicks leotarded in black, bongoed the night through in North Beach and Greenwich Village. The button-down minds at *Time* broke out an arsenal of alliteration and trained it on the Beats: They were, for starters, the "mendicants of marijuana and mad verse." The newsweekly took special aim not just at Kerouac's "soapless saga," but at Allen Ginsberg's "effete epic, *Howl*." They were doubtless familiar with Ginsberg's poem, "America," in which he apostrophizes: "Are you going to let your emotional life be run by Time Magazine?"

Yet if Kerouac's purported hipster values were attacked by *Time* and a welter of Establishment luminaries, they were championed by those urbane outlaws, Norman Mailer and Henry Miller. Indeed, Kerouac was swept up in a tide of attention. He became a matinee idol of sorts: He was the brains behind Presley's pelvis and Brando's sneer. His craggy visage was beamed coast to coast with TV personalities John Wingate, Mike Wallace, Jack Paar. He was asked by Lillian Hellman to write a play; he cut long-playing records, accompanied by Steve Allen and Zoot Sims; he spoke *ex cathedra* from the pages of *Playboy*, *Holiday*, and *Esquire*; and his agent reportedly turned down lucrative offers for the movie rights to *On the Road*.

Everyone wanted a piece of the "King of the Beats." Men in bars sought to try his macho with their knuckles. Friend and fellow novelist John Clellon Holmes recalls that women approached Kerouac's lover at the time and said, "Look, you're with him. You're twenty years old, but I've only got so many years left. I've got to fuck him now."

"Read his book," Holmes said to the multitudes who sought introductions to Kerouac. No, no, that wasn't it. They wanted to *experience* the man himself, to rub against his manna power. "He knows everything!" they said.

The irony in all this was that Kerouac knew somewhat less than everything. Everybody assumed that he was *On the Road*'s frenetic hero, the hip Noble Savage Dean Moriarty, when in truth he was Sal Paradise, the rather square and inhibited narrator, the diffident camp follower who threw the fabulous Moriarty into 3-D relief. Dean Moriarty *was* an actual person, as were all Kerouac's "fictional" characters. His real name was Neal Cassady, a name known at the time to few outside the Beat cadre, a name still to be fully reckoned with.

Neal Cassady was the muse of the Beat Generation. A blocked writer (with a fragmentary, posthumously published autobiography to his credit), he was the motive force behind Kerouac's bittersweet tale of two picaros alone with America. He was, in addition, "N. C., the secret hero" of Allen Ginsberg's "Howl," the anything-but-"effete epic" which, with its no-holds barred confessionalism, changed the direction of modern poetry. For a period in the late forties, both Kerouac and Ginsberg trailed Cassady around with their notebooks open, their pens at ready, charting not just his doings and sayings but their own sensations and progress in breaking free of middle-class hang-ups about sex, work, morality itself. Cassady entertained, perplexed, and amazed them—especially Ginsberg, who, initially reluctant to dispense with conventional ambitions, attempted against huge odds to channel Cassady's headlong energies. "We sit on the bed, cross-legged, facing each other. I have finally taught Dean [Neal] that he can do anything he wants, become mayor of Denver, marry a millionairess, or become the greatest poet since Rimbaud. But he keeps rushing out to see the midget auto races. I go with him."

Sometime during the postwar years, Joan Didion has noted, it became obvious that "the narrative on which many of us grew up no longer applies." The disjunctive agency was, of course, the Bomb, the example of Hiroshima and Nagasaki. "If the fate of twentieth-century man is to live with death from adolescence to premature senescence," wrote Norman Mailer just months before the publication of *On the Road*, "why then the only life-giving answer is to accept the terms of death, to live with death as an immediate danger, to divorce oneself from society, to exist without roots, to set out on that uncharted journey with the rebellious imperatives of the self. In short, whether the life is criminal or not, the decision is to encourage the psychopath in oneself..."

Mailer's famous essay "The White Negro," a brief for the replenishment of the self through antisocial means, was a virtual invocation of Neal Cassady. Not that

Cassady needed to encourage the psychopath in himself.
Quite the opposite: He was (to the extent such language
is helpful, and not merely reductive) a *natural*, not a
*philosophic* psychopath. He was incapable of sublima-
tion, of foregoing pleasure in the present in the interest
of "building a future." To say the least, he did not think
in terms of careers. Only the most marginal physical
work engaged him: being a railroad brakeman, a parking
lot attendant, a tire recapper—ostensibly plodding work
that he turned into intricate heroic labor with a comic
flair, as if Mack Sennett were recreating the cleansing of
the Augean stables. Cassady did not have to learn, in
Mailer's words, "to exist without roots," for he came of
age in a Denver flophouse. He did not have to scratch
deep for the "criminal" in himself, for by his late teens
he had stolen ("borrowed," he would say) hundreds of
cars. Nor did he have to disburden himself of sexual
scruple; in fact, when his first wife, LuAnne, met the
teen-aged Cassady, he was living with and servicing three
women—a daughter, her mother, and septuagenarian
grandmother. Cassady did not merely "live with death as
an immediate danger," but purposely put himself into
the destructive element, whether by driving cars at great
speeds in circumscribed conditions or by belaboring his
stone-hard physique with more sex, more stress, and,
finally, more drugs than any body should have to bear.
Neal Cassady lived in "the enormous present" of the
existentialists; he was Mailer's White Negro raised expo-
nentially. As Dean Moriarty, he was hugely attractive to
countless alienated and emotionally hamstrung young

men and women. In memoirist Aram Saroyan's phrase, he cast a "come-hither look" at a whole generation.

There was, however—as there usually is with superheroes—another, less than mythic aspect to Cassady. During the fifties he lived in a modest ranch-style house in Los Gatos, California, a small town near San Jose. He lived there with his second, resilient wife, Carolyn, and their three children. For years during the fifties Cassady attempted with little success to control the dictates of his body, the ceaseless injunctions to move, to do drugs, to fuck, to match strides with time itself. He was attempting to control his peculiar chemistry in 1958 when he was busted for drugs and sent to prison. Neat but sad irony, he was trying to lead the suburban life of Riley even as young Americans all across the country were disavowing Levittowns of the spirit in the name of that "new American saint," Dean Moriarty.

There are, despite reports to the contrary, second acts in American life and literature. Out of prison and on parole in the early sixties, Cassady started spending time in the Palo Alto area, where Stanford University is located. There he met novelist Ken Kesey and a band of prehirsute Golden Age hippies with names like Mountain Girl, the Hermit, Hassler, Zonker, Wavy Gravy, Stark Naked, Captain Trips (a roster familiar to readers of Tom Wolfe's *The Electric Kool-Aid Acid Test*). Cassady, the legendary driver of *On the Road*, was behind the wheel in 1964 when the Merry Pranksters took their meta-grotesque Day-Glo painted bus, "Furthur," on an epochal cross-country journey—a magical mystery tour that with

Dean Moriarty at the controls symbolically linked the countercultures of the fifties and the sixties. With Kerouac and Ginsberg, Cassady was an *enfant terrible*; with Kesey and Co. he was a *monstre sacré*.

It is fitting that Cassady, who came to be known as Speed Limit, was born in transit. On February 8, 1926, his father, Neal Sr., merely pulled off the road in Salt Lake City long enough for his bride, Maude, to make the delivery and briefly recuperate in a hospital near the Mormon Tabernacle. He then took a new bead on their destination, Hollywood.

It was a second marriage for Maude, a farm girl from outside Duluth, Minnesota, who at age thirteen was sent to work as a maid for a prominent family in Sioux City, Iowa. Enraptured by her beauty and delicacy, the family treated her as a daughter and thereby enabled her marriage in 1906 to James Kenneth Daly. A wealthy, prototypal Irish politico, Daly became mayor of Sioux City, only to die in office in 1922, leaving behind their seven children. At odds with her mother-in-law, Maude repaired to Des Moines, which brought her into the orbit of Neal Sr., a man in his early thirties with a history of failure and flight who was enjoying an *annus mirabilis*. In 1925 the former drunkard and park-bench vagrant was managing the top barbershop in the city and was, in a small way, cutting something of a social figure. He met and pursued Maude at the Des Moines Country Club. Within a short time they were married. Almost imme- diately, in an act of what his son later called "unaccountable constructiveness, neither anticipated nor repeated," Neal Sr. bought a Ford truck and set to building a house on its two-ton bed. It was in this bizarre house-truck that the couple, accompanied by Maude's two youngest children—the other five were left to shift for themselves—took off for Hollywood in the dead of winter and pulled from the road in Salt Lake City to give birth to Neal Sr.'s only son and namesake.

The newlyweds did reach Hollywood. Their prospects looked good when they bought a barbershop at the corner of Hollywood and Vine. But before long Neal Sr. had regressed to form: He was closing up the shop and drinking himself stupid for days at a time. Finally in 1928 they sold the business for a fraction of its value and moved to Denver, where the lawns were invitingly green and Maude had a brother. Neal Sr. was working something of a comeback in 1929 (he was financially abetted by Maude's boys Bill, age twenty-one, Ralph, eighteen, and Jack, sixteen, who had joined them and were bootlegging liquor) when the Crash occurred and completely undid him. The marriage limped on until 1932, when Maude and ten-year-old Jimmy and baby Shirley, Cassady's only full sibling, moved into a red brick apartment building, The Snowdon, located on an old inner-city block. It was then that big Neal and little Neal, age six, moved to a flophouse on the corner of Sixteenth and Market streets, the slums of the city.

The Metropolitan was a five-story condemned building with a clientele of winos and derelicts, obsequious, soft-brained men who lived by begging on the

main thoroughfares. There were no rooms per se, but
cubicles—thirty to forty sleeping cells priced at ten and
twenty-five cents a night. The child Neal and his father
resided in one of the two-bit cells, for which they paid
one dollar a week since they agreed to a third party, who
occupied a makeshift platform on a protruding pipe
elbow. Shorty was able to manage this abbreviated space
because he was a double amputee. He was, Neal recalled
in the autobiographical fragments of *The First Third*, an
extremely ugly but gentle soul "encrusted with dirt ...
with no-forehead face full of grinning rubber mouth that
showed black stubbed teeth." He had a slim torso and
oversized arms, which, blocks of wood in hand, he used
each day to propel a dolly to his post in front of the
relatively swell Manhattan Restaurant on Larimer Street.
There he would beg just enough to purchase the cheapest
rotgut, return to the cubicle, and drink himself to sleep.
Failing the accumulation of alms for oblivion, Shorty
would ease his burden by masturbating, often within
view of six-year-old Neal ("I thought it fried eggs littering
the floor.").

Typically, young Cassady would rise each morning
with the peal of the clock tower on the Daniels and
Fisher department store. Leaving his father groggy in
their sheetless bed, he would join a handful of men in
the sunlit lavatory, many of whom would be fighting the
shakes and would not chance shaving. Coffee, bread, and
oatmeal could be had at the Citizen's Mission, which
served breakfast and dinner to two hundred men, in
return for attendance at semi-weekly religious services.

Then Neal was off to school, which was over a mile away and within the district that embraced The Snowdon. School was apparently untraumatic for Neal, not even particularly noteworthy. More memorable was the trek to school, which he turned into complex adventure. There were the perilous shortcuts up fire escapes of slum buildings, across roofs, through alleys, by "haunted" houses; and the demanding feats of agility and endurance and will, tightroping across stretches of raised sidewalk, getting water from tall fountains without wetting shoes, holding the breath while traversing one hundred yards of blacktop at breakneck speed even while bouncing a ubiquitous dirty tennis ball, the whole business timed to the second so to arrive just as the school bell rang. "This running habit became so strong," he would say, "that I made it a habit never to walk out-of-doors, unless forced to do so by an accompanying adult."

Not school, which he attended through eighth grade (and sporadically thereafter), but The Metropolitan was his preferred environment. The flophouse habitués tended to be kind to "the barber's boy," since he served as a sop for their disappointment, as a stimulus to the visions of lost innocence to which they daily resorted. During the evening the inner lobby would come alive with a constant round of cards—casino, can-can, pieute, pinochle, poker. Little Neal would weave buoyantly in and out of the dim conviviality, playing with his home-made dart, a sewing needle stuck in a wooden match and with newspaper strips for feathers. Empty chairs, cracks in the floor, scum marks were his targets.

Saturday was much anticipated. It was when Neal Sr. worked the third chair at the Zaza barbershop on Larimer Street, and when young Neal luxuriated in the sweet smell of hair pomade and talcum powder while fingering through recent issues of *Liberty* magazine or the *Rocky Mountain News*. Next door was the filthy, rankly scented Zaza Theater at whose Saturday morning show Neal was a regular. He saw mostly westerns, Tim McCoy epics, Astaire and Rogers movies, monster flicks. "King Kong plays Ping-Pong with his ding dong" was a rhyme he picked up from the other kids. Saturday meant a midday meal at Mac's Lunch, a locally famous greasy spoon. It also meant the Saturday night drunk: the two Neals attending the midnight show at the Zaza, big Neal seeking solace in a bottle, little Neal finding his in *The Count of Monte Cristo*, his all-time favorite picture.

Sunday was little Neal's day. With the advent of spring, father and son would descend into the great, mysterious country below the Denver bowery. They would go down from Market to Wynkoop Street, past the American Furniture Company warehouse, the Singer Sewing Machine plant, the Great Western Sugar building, past the Union Train Station, skirting the railroad wonders of First through Fourteenth streets. Their destination? The "beach" of the South Platte River where it curled beneath the iron and wood bridge at Fifteenth Street. For hours on end Neal would sail rocks across the surface of the water. He would work at this skill for years, until eventually, in his teens, he could consistently get close to twenty skips in a single throw. It was perhaps the first of his obsessively attained, hyperkinetic and unmarketable skills, the most famous of which—his virtual emblem in his later years—was hammer flipping.

While the forays to the South Platte had their rustic aspect, they served to introduce Cassady to the netherbelly of the city. Searching along the shorelines, in the culverts, and under bridges for recyclable trash, which he would collect in a gunnysack and sell for a pittance to addicts on Larimer Street, he became something of a connoisseur of waste. This passion for "junking" familiarized him, however, not just with the dregs but with the substructure of Denver as well. He was fascinated by the miniworld of the railroad, the roundhouse, loading docks, cranes. And his dreams during this period turned on his discovery of the Public Service Company power plant and, most especially, of the innards of the Pride of the Rockies flour mill. "These dreams," he recalled in *The First Third*, "were filled with the geography of the [flour mill] building. It had a spacious basement floor that rose three stories with narrow cement ledges jutting out and many iron catwalks laced over its sides. The upperfloors had huge overhanging machines gathered so close that all the pathways were mere tunnels, even to one my size. Squares were cut in the concrete to allow enormous chainbelts to extend in mighty webs of leather through all the mill."

In this description and others, Cassady shows a genuine feel for mechanical ecologies. His rendering proceeds, however, to a Gothic eeriness: "Over the disarrayed

broken machinery parts ... and over all the dormant
building itself was the accumulated dust of a score years.
Hauntingly, it was a dead dust, though it lay ankle-deep
no speck ever rose to filter inside my shoes as I wandered
about in my amazed somnolency. Everything was dead—
still, no activity and no sound, save one thing: hundreds
of solar-energized flies buzzed over me. I felt in a tomb,
so isolated was I by the thick walls from rumbling 20th
Street viaduct, only yards away. Also and most oppressive
was the certainty that the summer heat would intensify
until in time its ebulliency became too entire to ever
again escape."

Kerouac would often refer to Cassady's
"sepulchral" nature, to the bleak subterranean portion of
his sensibility that made the visible, dynamic, and life-
affirming side all the more compelling. Clearly the prospect of the intensifying summer heat, the prospect of
continuing in a quasi-visionary state of "amazed somnolency," is not entirely oppressive. It had, for Cassady,
its own alluring "ebulliency."

The flour-mill episode is complemented in *The
First Third* by another recurrent dreamlike experience
with the felt conviction of a primal scene. Sometime in
the midthirties, Cassady's half brothers, Jack and Ralph,
decided that Neal should move into The Snowdon to live
with his mother; Jimmy, age twelve; and Shirley, age
three. The brothers, who used to beat up their pathetic
stepfather when he came home drunk were model bullies
for Jimmy, who took keen pleasure in drowning cats in
the toilet. Half his age, Neal was made to order for

Jimmy, whose most horrifying gambit was to force him
onto the family bed, a wall bed that pulled out horizon-
tally from beneath a cupboard, and then to deposit both
bed and brother back in the wall. Although Mrs. Cassady
was generally—obliviously—on hand, Neal never
screamed for fear that Jimmy would later get him and
for fear that he would use his store of oxygen and
suffocate as in a horror film at the Zaza.

There was a third reason, however. He rather
enjoyed the sensation of being in the wall. It did not
matter that he had less than a foot of clearance, nor that
he was often interred for upwards of an hour. The
experience had its own Poe-esque appeal. There would
begin a scrambling of the senses caused, he imagined, by
an "off balanced wheel whirling" inside his skull, which
"while slowly increasing in tempo set up a loose fan-like
vibration as it rotated into ever-tightening flutter." What
happened was that time in his head gradually tripled its
ordinary speed. The result was a "strangely pleasant, yet
disturbing enough to frighten, quickening of the brain's
action which resisted any rigorous attempt to throw it off
and return to normal-headedness."

It was, in short, much the same heightened
experience that Cassady would seek—what wife Carolyn
called his "courtship of death"—for the rest of his life. It
inadvertently recalled the oriental practice of *zazen* (literally, "wall gazing"), in which the mind is emptied of
content and repopulated with hypnagogic hallucinations.
It was as well, and more prophetically, a version of the

"systematic derangement of the senses" that the Beats would one day venerate in Rimbaud. Finally, it was a preview of the psychic dislocations that the Merry Pranksters would achieve several decades later through LSD.

Embedded in the wall at age seven, as if in a morgue drawer, Cassady was the fool of time, which accelerated at whim. Years later, after much experimentation with drugs, he would learn "to hold as still as death," to attend the leverlike flips of mind that signaled that time's torrent was speeding him past all thought to a space crowded with parti-colored images. He would discover that by strong concentration he could deflect the time quickening, even momentarily hold and analyze the "headspins." "We all *know* Time!" was his refrain as Cody Pomeray or Dean Moriarty in Kerouac's books.

Jimmy would continue for more than a year to incarcerate Neal in his mattressed jail. After a while the anticipated event must have taken on the quality of rite or serial ordeal. Indeed, the pattern recalls, on however modest a scale, those legendary stories in which the hero only half voluntarily descends to the underworld, to the womb/tomb or World Navel, in order to emerge cleansed and with new powers which he uses to the benefit of humanity. One day Jack Kerouac would pledge, through his books, to "redeem life from darkness." Naturally, Kerouac had his own peculiar story and reason for making the pledge. Yet there is little doubt that his inspiration and model was Neal Cassady. Cassady's lifelong heroism consisted precisely in redeeming life from darkness, in the descent into and the return from the abyss. His many admirers would say that he made his voyage into the dark for all of us.

During the next six or seven years, into his early teens, Neal would summer with his father. He would join big Neal in several thousand-mile jaunts through the West, hitchhiking, riding the rails, frequenting hobo jungles in California, selling homemade flyswatters in Nebraska. He would sleep in cardboard cartons in boxcars and in a rolltop desk on Larimer Street. He would learn his first con-man tricks, notably how to affect the waif look so to better cadge nickels for his father and cronies to convert into wine, canned heat (denatured alcohol), even bay rum.

By age nine he had had his full sexual initiation. By then he'd had the usual interludes with slightly older girls who led him in genital show and tell, and he'd permitted at least one older boy to "drink the water" from his "pee pee." But he came sexually of age under the auspice of his father, and under circumstances that were typically outré. One evening the two Neals went home with a feeble-minded German drinking buddy who lived, with his large family, in a barn in southwest Denver. There, as if in a scene from Jerzy Kosinski's *The Painted Bird*, little Neal looked on as the German's numerous sons smoked, cussed, fought, and generally raised the level of their savagery. Finally, sucked into the riot, nine-year-old Neal followed the oldest brother in mounting all the sisters small enough to hold down. It

was no wonder that, in full maturity, Cassady was never
able to totally credit the idea of rape.

The move to The Snowdon was in no sense a
pastoral or even suburban retreat. Rather it was a move
to a more efficient degeneracy. Bums were exchanged for
sharpers. There were a few pious families in the shabby
four-story Victorian building, but the residence was notorious for its cast of ex-cons, perverts, prostitutes, addicts.
And in the basement, figuratively pumping bellows, were
small-time mafiosi Ralph and Jack, who ran a pack of
kids that stole and extorted and played havoc with the
neighborhood.

Given this milieu, it is not surprising that by his
late teens Cassady had been arrested by the police ten
times, convicted six times, and had served a year and
some months in jail. The nature of his "criminality" is
worth remarking, however; his crimes were not violent
ones, as were brother Jimmy's, nor was he, like Ralph
and Jack, a racketeer. His lovemaking a question apart,
Cassady came to abhor violence at an early age. For one
thing, he had before him the example of his father, who
was esteemed at The Metropolitan for his gentle nature.
Then, too, Jimmy all but schooled him in pacifism by
forcing him to fight with other kids throughout his
childhood. Neal was always the youngest and smallest in
a volatile world of desperate men and men-children. He
would later say that he learned as early as age three or
four that competition with others was unavailing: It only
brought on potentially violent situations. He learned,
instead, to compete with himself, to test his own limits,

and to gratify his senses in the process. Neal "the criminal" was a car thief who stole, by his reckoning, five hundred vehicles during adolescence. Yet he pinched the cars for the sensation, not for secular profit. He was a joyrider in the strict sense of the word.

Cassady was not immoral so much as amoral. Sex and stealing worked off and pleasured the same circuit. Both activities courted death, naturally, and the more intricate the arrangements and the greater the difficulty, the more profound the rush, the greater the ebulliency. Neal's pleasure in sex was not, however, unalloyed, especially in later years. It was tinged with psychodrama, in which he often cast his lover of the moment as a temptress leading him to iniquity. Several of his women would later attribute his "worm of guilt" to his belated introduction into Roman Catholicism. Neal was baptized at age ten and served for three years, the crucial years of puberty, as an altar boy at Holy Ghost Church, where his godfather was a priest. In *The First Third* Cassady would recall that he was, for a time, utterly absorbed by the lives of the saints, and that he even thought to become a Christian Brother, until he abruptly disappeared "down the pleasanter path of evil."

Sex had its practical aspect as well. Never having much in the way of goods or social leverage, Cassady employed sex as his prime currency of exchange. At age twelve he was screwing an imbecile maid in a well-furbished house to win his dinner. In his twenties, and on the road with Kerouac, he was performing truck-stop quickies with homosexuals in trade for rides. Kerouac often referred to Cassady's "flirtatious eyes" and "fluttering lashes." His every relationship was suffused with a kind of erotic intensity.

In October 1942, for example, fifteen-year-old Neal, dressed in dungarees, shoes without socks, khaki Army shirt, entered a pool hall in downtown Denver and made what Kerouac called "the first great con man proposition of his life." For some weeks he had been visiting the pool hall and studying most particularly a physically unprepossessing billiards virtuoso of approximately his own age. Finally he approached Jim Holmes (Tom Watson in *Visions of Cody*) and saturated him with the flood of verbiage for which he would become famous. The mad gist of it was that he would tutor Holmes in the niceties of philosophy and literature if Holmes would agree to coach him in rotation pool, snooker, nine ball. Holmes was bewildered, intrigued, flattered by the fifteen-minute assault that included, among other full-tilt propositions, the idea that Neal commandeer a vehicle and whisk Holmes and friends off to see the next day's Notre Dame football game a thousand miles away. What was Holmes to do? Not knowing Cassady, and never before (or since) having seen his like, he rather sensibly assumed that Neal's spate of language derived from an empty stomach. He took the youthful con man home for a square meal, and ended up teaching him how to cheat at cards, giving him a brown tweed suit (Neal's first), as well as a place to live, at Neal's wish, for the next four years.

"It's awful hard to explain Neal," Holmes would say years later to Kerouac biographers Barry Gifford and Lawrence Lee in *Jack's Book*, "because you just don't run into people like that. You just never see them, somebody who is willing to give their undivided attention for hours at a time. How many people do you ever know that will do that?"

Implausible as it may seem, Cassady probably had the wherewithal to acquaint Jim Holmes with at least the bare bones of philosophy and literature, for he'd been training himself in The Great Books. (His favorites were, significantly, Schopenhauer and Proust: the philosopher who portrayed man as a creature of will and desire rather than intellect; the novelist who fabricated a world of sensation and pure consciousness, who measured time not by the clock but on the pulse.) In the fall of 1942 when he laid siege to Holmes, Cassady was recently returned from a stint in reform school. While there, he had a dream that changed his life. He dreamed of a huge flophouse dormitory, curiously (but suggestively) located in a Denver high school auditorium. In the dream he was no longer a young man but was in his forties, wearing a ragged T-shirt and a beer belly. His hair was thin, his face was puffy, he was missing a tooth, and he was going somewhere to sell the mattress under his arm for wine money. Suddenly his father materialized, wearing his old black baseball cap; he was typically bedraggled and atypically fitted with a convulsive erection. Neal Sr. wanted in on the profits from the mattress sale and ran after his fleeing son, who awoke with his stomach in turmoil.

That very day a deeply affected Neal decided on a course of self-improvement that reads like a parody of a regimen conceived by Ben Franklin, or like the schedule

inscribed by F. Scott Fitzgerald's James Gatz on the inside
cover of a book titled, too appropriately, *Hopalong Cas-
sidy*. Home from reform school, Neal arose each morning
at seven. At seven-fifteen, he washed at the Zaza barbershop sink, then delivered his paper route. At nine he
won his breakfast from the demented maid or, failing
that, from a second miss named Cherry Mary. At ten he
joined the staff in opening the public library and read
Schopenhauer, *et al*. Eleven found him washing and
parking cars at the Rocky Mountain Garage. At noon he
borrowed a bike to pedal five miles into the country to
lunch with friends and their families (he generally stayed
to do chores), after which he returned to the library for
further bouts with philosophy and literature. At four he
headed for the pool hall and rest and relaxation, which
in turn led to twilight baseball and/or other evening
amusements. At eleven he pilfered coins from a news-
stand to purchase a bowery beef stew, then found a place
to sleep, maybe a bathtub in the Greeley Hotel.

It was about this time, too, that Neal met Justin
Brierly, a Denver high school teacher, lawyer, property
owner, and civic bigwig. One day Brierly was inspecting
one of his rent houses and came upon Cassady, rather
startingly, in a hallway. Neal was naked, fresh from
coitus with the imbecile maid. Their conversation was
reportedly brief, and as follows. Neal, indignant: "How
did you get in here?" Brierly, brandishing a key: "I'm
sorry, this is my house."

In any case, Brierly soon became Cassady's mentor. He is called Denver D. Doll in *On the Road* and
Justin B. Mannerly in the Cassady-Ginsberg letters, but it

is clear that Neal was, for a time, much impressed by the older man and eager to please him with intellectual accomplishments. More importantly, Brierly was the means by which Cassady came into contact with the cream of Denver youth, several of whom attended Columbia College in New York City. He was, as well, Neal's sponsor and sole correspondent when, in 1944, he was sent once more to do time at the state reformatory in Buena Vista.

During the summer of 1945, not long after returning from Buena Vista, Neal strolled one day into Walgreen's drugstore in Denver and—accompanied by Jeannie, his woman and benefactress of the moment—pointed to a blonde-haired "bluebell of a girl" sitting in one of the booths and stated, "That's the girl I'm going to marry." He'd never met LuAnne Henderson, who was age fifteen to his nineteen, but he had been keenly aware of her for some time. On August 1 they were married: with LuAnne eluding a stepfather who was finding her striking physical development increasingly tempting, and with Neal becoming a second-story man in order to abscond with his clothes and books from Jeannie's house, where he had continued to live while paying clandestine court to LuAnne.

The newlyweds quickly took to the road, hitch-hiking to Nebraska, where LuAnne found work as a housekeeper for a blind lawyer and Neal got a job as a dishwasher. They lived in a single room, paying twelve dollars a month rent, and at night Neal read aloud (and explicated) Shakespeare and his beloved Proust. Eventually they moved on to Sidney, Nebraska, where LuAnne kept house for an aunt who worked her "like a horse."

Late in 1946, seeing LuAnne on her knees scrubbing the front porch during a blizzard, Neal decided that they had had enough of the Midwest. LuAnne promptly went upstairs and took three hundred dollars.
Neal clipped the uncle's car, and they were off. They thought, first, to stop at a friend's ranch in Sterling, Colorado; then, with Neal leaning out of the passenger-side window, a handkerchief tied around his eyes in order to see through the sleet, they decided to make straight for New York. They hoped to catch up with two of Brierly's prize charges who were studying at Columbia College: Hal Chase and Ed White. They hoped, too, to finally meet Chase and White's storied poet friends, Allen Ginsberg and Jack Kerouac.

# PART TWO

# DEAN MORIARTY

*Perhaps you are a temptation rather than
an angel.
Yet you have a star in your forehead....*

ALLEN GINSBERG in a letter to Neal Cassady, August 1948

In 1946 Jack Kerouac and Allen Ginsberg were at critical
pauses in their lives. Each had attended Columbia College, and still lived mostly in the Morningside Heights
area. Each had felt smothered by academia, had bridled
against authority and left under a cloud—Kerouac giving
up possible stardom on the nationally renowned football
team, Ginsberg precluding a career in law and labor
politics inspired by Eugene V. Debs, the Wobblies, Sacco
and Vanzetti. Superficially they were very different people. Kerouac was the big bluff jock (an "Arrow-collar ad
type," one friend said), a Canuck Roman Catholic from
Lowell, Massachusetts. Ginsberg was the skinny Jewish
kid with black-rimmed glasses and protruding ears, "an
inquisitive dormouse" (in John Clellon Holmes's phrase)
from Paterson, New Jersey. Yet they were profoundly
alike. Each had a father who'd fared poorly with the
System but nevertheless preached conventional success.
Each had a disfiguring oedipal relationship with his
mother. Each felt haunted, sullied: Jack by the saintly
image of Gerard, his older brother, who died of rheumatic fever at age nine; Allen by his burgeoning
homosexuality.

31

Neither Kerouac nor Ginsberg fit in, and they gravitated toward persons similarly estranged. Indeed, their friends were a virtual register of their frustrations and desires, and an index to the attitudes they coveted. Especially notable were Lucien Carr, Bill Cannastra, William S. Burroughs, and Herbert Huncke.

Lucien Carr was a strikingly handsome aristocrat from St. Louis with blond hair and green catlike eyes, with the enviable looks and manner of Rimbaud. Carr was cynical, smart-ass. He was fond of Pernod, of exercrating the hoi polloi, and of what André Gide called *actes gratuits*, startling gestures that revealed him as at once impulsive and contrary, artificial and authentic—in short, as deep-souled.

In the summer of 1944 Carr and Kerouac planned to ship out of New York as common seamen, their destination France, never mind the war. "We'll land at the second front," said the Carr character in Kerouac's *Vanity of Duluoz*. "We'll walk to Paris: I'll be a deaf mute and you speak country French and we'll pretend we're peasants. When we get to Paris it will probably be on the verge of being liberated. We'll find symbols saturated in the gutters of Montmartre. We'll write poetry, paint, drink red wine, wear berets. I feel like I'm in a pond that's drying out and I'm about to suffocate. I s'pose you understand."

Of course Kerouac understood. Yet Carr was not merely referring to the ennui they shared, but to his peculiar plight. He meant David Kammerer, the tall, red-bearded older man who had been pursuing Lucien for years, shamelessly following him from school to school, from St. Louis to Massachusetts to Maine to Illinois and now to New York, where he found work as a janitor. Kammerer was hopelessly in love with the incorrigibly heterosexual Carr, and had taken to stealing into Lucien's apartment during the night and staring long and intently at his sleeping beloved. The evening of the day that Carr and Kerouac attempted, unsuccessfully, to ship for France, Carr went down by the Hudson River with Kammerer and stabbed him to death with a Boy Scout knife. The details of the killing were muddled, but the *Daily News* billed it as an "honor slaying," and Carr served two years for manslaughter. "To plunge to the bottom of the abyss," Rimbaud wrote. "Heaven or Hell, what matter?"

Carr was a school chum with a set of gaudily attractive stances. He would, understandably, be chastened by the Kammerer episode. Less co-optable—unredeemable, finally—was Bill Cannastra, the cynosure of "subterraneans" in young alienated New York. He was an Ivy League law school dropout who sometimes worked in a bakery. He was a master of antirevels notorious for streaking naked through Village streets at three in the morning, for dancing on shattered glass to Bach fugues, for planting a wet kiss on an unsuspecting marine in the White Rose Bar. Drinking was his vocation, brutal sarcasm his metier, self-abuse his element. He made Carr look like a piker.

Cannastra's downtown loft, littered with broken records, yellowed mattresses, slashed car seats, was a

mecca for the lost, for those who craved undifferentiated
excess, for those who felt stirrings they didn't quite
understand or fully credit. As one character says in *GO*,
John Clellon Holmes's *roman à clef*: "Don't you know that
people who can't believe in anything else always believe
in Bill?" Their belief was necessarily short-lived, for the
"church" foundered in 1950 when Cannastra tried to
climb out a subway window just as the train was leaving
the station and was decapitated. It was a suitably gratuitous end to a short, furiously emblematic life.

Less spectacular, perhaps, was the darkly brilliant
William S. Burroughs. Grandson to the man who per-
fected the adding machine and typically dressed in a
worn Chesterfield coat and bowler, Burroughs was a
"patrician thin-lipped Harvard grad" who seemed to have
built a life of renunciations. He was, in the nice sense of
the word, a dandy: He made of himself a spare "work of
art" shaped in contradistinction to bourgeois value. He
was homosexual. He was a junkie for fifteen years. He
worked the hole out of Times Square—that is, he rolled
drunks in the subway with a small-time criminal associate, not out of need but for the experience. Burroughs
was a complex personality. In part, he purposely formu-
lated a counter-aesthetic of the ugly and outrageous to
purge himself of discredited twentieth-century human-
ism. In greater part, he was searching through the nether
world of drugs and crime for the identity he felt had
been denied him by the "WASP elite." He had been
ostracized since childhood by midwestern toffs who
likened him, in his presence, to a "walking corpse" or
"sheep-killing dog." He had subsequently been rejected

most every way he turned—by the clubs at Harvard, the
O.S.S., the Navy.

Burroughs was loyal, compassionate, even tender
to Kerouac and Ginsberg, who were a dozen years his
junior. He was their Vergil, introducing them to a range
of unsettling writers and ideas, to Céline, Genet, Kafka,
Wilhelm Reich, Cocteau on opium, Spengler's *Decline of
the West*, Count Korzybski's *Science and Sanity*. He introduced them as well to his morphine connection, Herbert
Huncke, an emaciated hustler with saucer-big brown eyes
who quivered involuntarily and wore pancake makeup to
cover his drug-mottled skin.

"My measure [of a person's worth] at the time,"
Ginsberg would say, "was the sense of personal genius
and acceptance of all strangeness in people as their
nobility." The strangeness, the noble marginality of the
Times Square hipsters, entranced Kerouac and Ginsberg.
"They looked like criminals," Kerouac would recall a
decade later in *Playboy*, "but they kept talking about the
same things I liked, long outlines of personal experience
and visions, nightlong confessions full of hope that had
become illicit and repressed by War, stirrings, rumblings
of a new soul." Something was trying to get born in the
late forties. A new consciousness was germinating in the
human refuse in the gloom of the Angle Bar on Eighth
Avenue and Forty-second Street, where Alfred Kinsey
conducted his famous interviews on sexual mores in the
Lower Depths.

"We went to Huncke," John Clellon Holmes would
say, "just because of the kind of life he had lived—he was
a source—even more, a model of how to survive." Huncke

was a furtive, sweet-souled junkie who introduced Kerouac and Ginsberg to life at ground zero. His Rx for
survival was, however, at least as debilitating as the
malady it purported to cure. Under Huncke's tutelage,
Kerouac's hair went thin and his hard physique pulpy
from too much Benzedrine. Eventually Ginsberg would
be arrested for harboring the Times Square hustler
(called Creep by the cops) and would be committed to
the Columbia Psychiatric Institute for eight months.

By the winter of 1946–47, the Beat pair was ready
for a change. They were ready to trade authentic despair
for manic ecstasy, "beaten-down" for "beatific." They
were primed, without knowing it, for Neal Cassady.

As it turned out, Cassady met Ginsberg first. The meet-
ing occurred more or less by accident late in 1946 at the
West End Bar, across the way from Columbia College.
Neal and LuAnne were with Hal Chase, who heard a
familiar voice in a nearby booth and simply called
Ginsberg over. From Allen's perspective, although he
knew of Cassady through ex-roommate Chase, Neal and
LuAnne were merely young marrieds looking for a pad.
He couldn't help them, and that was pretty much that.
Neal, meanwhile, saw Allen through a scrim of lurid
ideas gathered from Chase: Ginsberg was a homosexual
and a Jew "whose amazing mind had a germ of decay in
it and whose sterility had produced a blasé, yet fascinat-
ing mask." Neal regarded Allen warily, while Allen,
under the circumstances, scarcely regarded Neal at all.

The meeting with Kerouac was more eventful. Around Christmas, Kerouac went with Ed White and Hal Chase to visit the Denver *wunderkind* at a cold-water flat in Spanish Harlem. As wonted, Cassady greeted his visitors in the nude. "In the door he stood with a perfect build, large blue eyes full of questions, but already thinning in edges, at edges, into sly, or shy, or coy disbelief, not that he's coy or even demure." Cassady was hard-jawed, big-boned, sinewy but muscled, and he immediately struck Kerouac as the rugged and disreputable original of which the singing cowboy Gene Autry was a wholesome counterfeit. It was only 1947, but Neal was already seasoning his patter with manifold *yes*'s and *that's right*'s, even while bobbing up and down like a young boxer taking instructions, as if to give the impression that he was listening to every word, when in truth, it seemed to Kerouac, he was thinking solely of his next piece of ass, plotting it in his head while wife LuAnne, surprised by the visit, was over on the couch buttoning up from the last.

It was instantly apparent to Kerouac that sex was the one holy thing in Cassady's life. A distant second, clearly, was a need to be taken for someone of intellectual consequence, a need flagrant in his speech. "Yes, of course, I know exactly what you mean," he said when the conversation turned to writing. "And, in fact, all those problems have occurred to me, but the thing that I want is the realization of those factors that should depend on Schopenhauer's dichotomy for any inwardly realized..."

In the early days, Cassady was ambitious for worldly success, however rarefied. He aspired to be a writer, a poet. Back in Denver, pursuing his post-reform school course of self-improvement, he'd had a critical tête-à-tête with Hal Chase, who was then his ego ideal. He told Chase, by way of snowing him, that the most important person in the world, the one who really matters is the philosopher. No, said Chase, summarily. The poet counts much more than the philosopher. Thud! So much for Cassady's current regime, his assault on The Great Books. "I was so stupefied and astounded and nullified and disturbed that anyone could honestly believe that, that I, well I ... probably, I don't really want—care to speculate to say *why*, that the reason came about, but suddenly I realized that the philosopher was not—that the poet *was* more important than the philosopher."

Thus the impetus for the trip to New York was born of a pressing need to meet real poets, to meet Ginsberg and Kerouac. Thus, shortly after the initial meeting, Neal was hovering at Jack's shoulder as he was finishing a chapter of his first book, *The Town and the City*. Looking on as Kerouac typed his one hundred words a minute, Cassady riffed his encouragement, "Yes! That's right! Wow! Man!" and "Phew!" pausing only to wipe the sympathetic sweat from his face with a handkerchief.

"He was conning me and I knew it (for room and board and 'how-to-write,' etc.)," wrote Kerouac. "And he knew that I knew (this has been the basis of our relationship), but I didn't care and we got along fine."

There was no outright catering, but the relationship, freshly minted, retained a certain fragility. "We tiptoed around each other like heartbreaking new friends."

And soon Ginsberg was in the fold as well. On January 10 Kerouac took Cassady to the apartment of a friend in the East Eighties to smoke marijuana, an experience that had somehow eluded him. Ginsberg was present, and this time: ripeness was all. "Two piercing eyes glanced into two piercing eyes," Jack wrote in *On the Road*, "the holy con-man with the shining mind, and the sorrowful poetic con-man with the dark mind." From that moment forward Kerouac saw a good deal less of Cassady, and of Ginsberg too, for Allen and Neal embarked on a "tremendous season" together.

"I wanted to live in a big tragedy-comedy Dostoevskian universe," Ginsberg later told biographer Jane Kramer. "That was my ideal. A universe where the characters would all rush up and *confront* each other. A universe where everybody was involved in seeking God and all the heroes were holy idiots."

Clearly, Ginsberg's wishes were met in Cassady. Here was a slim-hipped hedonist who could throw a football seventy yards, do fifty chin-ups at a clip, and masturbate six times a day every day. Here was a man who had suffered a life at once blighted and intriguingly exotic and who was somehow all the more sensitive, sensual, and amorous for it. Here was a man who was as "criminal" and "marginal" as Huncke, but who was vastly more joyous and palatable, a man who was potentially as smart as Burroughs but who was natural, intuitive, intellectually unformed—who was, in a word, *radiant*.

Cassady was a "holy idiot," an *ignu* in Ginsberg parlance ("ignu is an angel in comical form"). He was, said Kerouac, conferring a valued honorific, "more like Dostoevsky than anyone I know." No experience, no pastime, no job could ever be casual to him. "The most fantastic parking lot attendant in the world, he can back a car forty miles an hour into a tight squeeze and stop at the wall, jump out, race among fenders, leap into another car, circle it fifty miles an hour into a narrow space, back swiftly into a tight spot, *hump*, snap the car with the emergency so that you can see it bounce as he flies out, then clear to the ticket shack, sprinting like a track star, hand in ticket, leap into a newly arrived car before the owner's half out, leap literally under him as he steps out, start the car with the door flapping and roar off to the next available spot, arc, pop in, brake, out, run; working like that without pause eight hours a night ... in greasy wino pants with a frayed fur-lined jacket and beat shoes that flap."

In the postwar years one wanted fervently to punch through the mummery of accepted social behavior, to participate (in Seymour Krim's phrase) "more Elizabethanly in this over-abundant life." Yet the problem was, to quote Robert Musil's *The Man Without Qualities*, "these days one never sees oneself whole and one never moves as a whole." That is, of course, unless "one" were Neal Cassady, for Cassady was deliciously all of a piece.

He drove a car, made love, listened to jazz, talked the
night through in the same "pious frenzy." His every act
was a revelation, an aggressive declaration of self. He
had, said Kerouac, the "energy of a new kind of American saint." It was no wonder, therefore, that Ginsberg,
who wanted dearly to be a saint—"I want to be a saint,
a real saint while I am young," he wrote mentor Mark
Van Doren, "for there is so much work to do"—fell
desperately in love with him.

This was not the same Allen Ginsberg who attained international celebrity during the sixties. This was
not the genial, self-possessed and woolly shaman who
chanted mantras to exorcise demons from the Pentagon,
who in 1965 was dubbed King of the May in Prague.
Rather, this was the pre-"Howl" Ginsberg who had not
yet learned to vilify America for its repressiveness and
his ills. This was the pre-expansive poet who imitated
sixteenth-century verse forms and wrote crabbed little
poems in a minor modern way. This was the troubled
young man revealed a decade later in the disturbingly
beautiful poem, "Kaddish." Above all, this was the son of
a mad idealist mother, Naomi Ginsberg, a thirties Com-
munist whose mind snapped irreparably, who was
convinced that President Roosevelt was "wire-tapping"
her head, who saw Hitler in her room and his mustache
in the sink. At age forty she paraded nude, thoughtlessly,
flirtatiously, before her twelve-year-old son, with her
operation scars tugging down in her fat "like hideous
thick zippers." She alternately berated and adored Allen.
She totally confused him, especially sexually.

Late one night in January, after days of racing
around "digging" the city and confronting each other like
Dostoevskian heroes, Cassady and Ginsberg found themselves at an all-night party on 104th Street. There were
not enough beds to go around, so they were forced to
double up. During the night, in an act of compassion and
gratitude more than desire, Neal pulled a trembling and
shame-ridden Allen to his side of the bed. A week later,
they exchanged vows to love one another. Ambivalent but
proud, Kerouac compared the two to Rimbaud and
Verlaine.

The madcap idyll lasted a couple of months
more, until Cassady, who had been deserted by the
thoroughly deserted LuAnne, decided to return to Denver.
From there he began an ambiguous correspondence.
Caught up again in his usual complex heterosexual
round, he wrote Allen that he feared he could not
continue their "affair," expecially in the "sacramental"
manner that Allen desired. "I really don't know how
much I can be satisfied to love you," he wrote. "I,
somehow, dislike pricks & men & before you, had
consciously forced myself to be homosexual, now, I'm not
sure whether with you I was not just forceing [sic] myself
unconsciously.... You meant so much to me, I now feel I
was forcing a desire for you bodily as a compansation
[sic] to you for all you were giving me."

Ginsberg was deeply hurt by Cassady's letters and,
in his anguish, wrote Neal accusing him of being a
"dirty, double crossing, faithless bitch." Cassady subsequently tried to explain the nature of his love, the extent

of his capacity for love. He wrote of an "objectivity of emotionality" that enabled him, ideally, "to move freely in each groove as it came." "The prime difference of our respective personalities is this [objectivity]," he said, "and once fully realized, will I hope, tend to weld us together, rather than be a cause for conflict."

Although it was an ideal as old in America as the Oneida Community, Cassady's ethic of free and groovy love would have to wait until the sixties to receive substantial cultural endorsement. In 1968 Ginsberg himself would come to sing of Neal's "Impersonal, tender" love. But in 1947 he was nowhere near that sort of disinterestedness. Besides, Cassady was less than candid with Ginsberg in his letters. In one missive he would seem to hold forth the possibility of their union; in the next he would recant. Neal was more than a little the cock tease and "faithless bitch." Allen was the most enthralling sensibility he'd ever known, and he was anxious to keep the relationship viable.

In the summer of 1947, against what should have been his better judgment, Ginsberg journeyed to Denver to be with his mercurial beloved. He arrived to find that Neal had not only patched matters with LuAnne but had fallen in love anew, heavily, with Carolyn Robinson. She was blonde, good-looking, refined, something of a "society girl." She had graduated from Bennington and was a teaching assistant pursuing a degree in theater arts at the University of Denver. She represented a challenge. In a sense, she was everything—or rather, half of everything—that Neal was seeking in his quest to transcend his dreary beginnings. Carolyn and Allen were object complements, social and intellectual imprimaturs, while LuAnne was a token of his past, a scarcely domesticated barbarian like himself.

Although in real life it caused more pain than pleasure, Cassady's summer schedule is treated brightly in *On the Road*. "The schedule is this," the Ginsberg character is made to say, "I came off work a half-hour ago. In that time Dean [Neal] is balling Marylou [LuAnne] at the hotel and gives me time to change and dress. At one sharp he rushes from Marylou to Camille [Carolyn]—of course neither one of them knows what's going on—and bangs her once, giving me time to arrive at one-thirty. Then he comes out with me—first he has to beg with Camille, who's already started hating me— and we come here to talk till six in the morning. We usually spend more time than that, but it's getting awfully complicated and he's pressed for time. Then at six he goes back to Marylou—and he's going to spend all day tomorrow running around to get the necessary papers for their divorce. Marylou's all for it, but she insists upon banging in the interim. She says she loves him—so does Camille." And so of course did Ginsberg, although *On The Road* shies from saying so and, thereby, from overtly treating homosexual love.

Nor does Kerouac's classic recount the moment when Neal's schedule exploded: when Carolyn walked into Cassady's rooming-house quarters and discovered Neal in bed with Allen and LuAnne. That morning an indignant Carolyn set off for California. Shortly thereafter

Allen and Neal left LuAnne in Denver and made their
way down to visit Burroughs on his ranch in Texas,
where he was living with wife Joan and children and
Huncke, far from the axis of what he considered the
American Police State. By that September it was clear
that Neal's repugnance to "pricks & men" could not be
overcome. He promised Ginsberg one last night in a
Houston hotel, which turned into a fiasco when Cassady,
high on assorted stuff, cut off in a jeep with a "mad
woman" only to return to the hotel where Ginsberg was
waiting and to burst in upon Huncke, who was trysting
with a young boy. Allen and Huncke fumed, and Neal
mercilessly passed out.

In storybook fashion, Ginsberg signed on a freigh-
ter bound for Africa and took his sick heart to sea. But it
would be years before he could fully clear himself of the
love-hate that he felt for Cassady. In the meantime he
wrote some extraordinary letters, which are gathered in
*As Ever*, the Cassady-Ginsberg correspondence. In one
letter in particular, in the fall of 1947, Allen reminds Neal
that he, Neal, initiated their love. "Don't you remember
how you made me stop trembling in shame and drew
me to you?" he asks. "Don't you know what I felt then, as
if you were a saint...?" He proceeds to make a close
reading of Neal's previous letter, hoping thereby to dis-
cern cause for optimism for their reunion. He includes
verses from a rather conventional poem of his own
making, which give tepid expression to his passion and
contrast wildly with what follows. He promises to grovel
at Neal's feet. He promises to perform any "indecencies"

Neal may wish. He cajoles and threatens and mocks. He waxes majestic: "Don't think that I forget myself, it is only that I have so much soul that I can rise above you not in mockery or mind but in spiritual genius...." In one stunning passage he plies a gamut of confused appeals: "And I will pay you back, you will see, you have never touched my intellect, I can teach you, really, what you want to know now, I will give you money. You know, or will someday learn, that you have no existence outside of me and never will be free until I free you."

The letter is a display worthy of Shakespeare's infinitely various Cleopatra, who might have joined Ginsberg in saying, "I am not so strong that I can afford to choose my weapons." The letter's publication stands as testament to Ginsberg's courageous honesty, to his subsequent vow to stand naked before the universe. "The point of Beat," Ginsberg would tell an interviewer in the late fifties, "is that you get beat down to a certain nakedness where you are actually able to see the world in a visionary way, which is the old classical understanding of what happens in the dark night of the soul."

Cassady was the entelechy, or vital force, that served to strip Ginsberg of his assorted assumptions and pretentions, to denude him of his "tenderest hopes," even his *hauteur.* It was a letter from Neal in May 1948 that finally tipped Allen over the edge into the abyss or "dark night of the soul." Lying in bed in his Harlem tenement, having read Cassady's letter, having just masturbated, Ginsberg heard "a very deep earthen grave voice in the room." It was the voice, he was certain, of the English visionary William Blake, whose poems were in his lap. It was as if God were speaking gravely and tenderly to his only son, speaking through Blake's poems—first, "Ah, Sun-flower!" then "The Sick Rose" and "The Little Girl Lost."

> Ah, Sun-flower, weary of time,
> Who countest the steps of the Sun,
> Seeking after that sweet golden clime,
> Where the traveller's journey is done.

The poem was a lightly coded message. It meant, a world-weary Ginsberg realized with a shudder, that there *was* a place, that there *was* a sweet golden clime. "I suddenly realized that *this* existence was *it!*" He suddenly realized that "Ah, Sun-flower!" was a sum of consolations and injunctions and that it was addressed to him! He promptly crawled out on the fire escape, tapped on the window of a pair of girls living next door, and shouted, "I've seen God!" Naturally, the girls banged the window shut.

It was only the beginning. In his despondency, he had written Kerouac that he was turning into one of those men who flashes his cock before juvenile delinquents. Now he wrote, "I have *seen* the Nightingale at last." For weeks Ginsberg would be rocked by revelations. The world had turned to glass, concealing nothing. Everywhere he went he saw "grotesques," the faces of "people twisted with rejection and hatred of self," mirror images of his own preregenerate self. He felt an immediate messianic calling to "break down everybody's masks and roles sufficiently so that everybody has to face the universe," so that everybody has to face the present Apocalypse: the prospect of the Bomb and the need to find, in Blake's words, "Eternity in an hour." A terrible beauty had been born. Cassady, the sepulchral "cocksman and Adonis from Denver," was forcing *him*, Ginsberg, to redeem life from darkness.

The letter that so affected Allen strikes a new note for Neal. On April Fools' Day 1948, Cassady married Carolyn Robinson, who would have a baby in the fall. Upon hearing of the event, Ginsberg wrote: "Now, I suppose I should congratulate you upon your marriage. So O.K. Pops everything you do is great." Missing, or ignoring, Ginsberg's bitter irony, Cassady replied from his new home in San Francisco: "Everything I do is not great. I've never done anything great. I see no greatness in my self. … I'm a simple-minded, child-like, insipid sort of moronic and kind of awkward feeling adolescent." Having been depressed for months, he suggested: "You should congratulate me—as you would congratulate me on, say, buying a car, or some such impersonal object." He closed the letter with: "Let us stop corresponding—I'm not the N.C. you knew. I'm not N.C. anymore. I more closely resemble Baudelaire."

More damaged angel than blithe spirit, this new and relatively nuanced Cassady was the one who spoke to Kerouac's peculiar set of facts and capitvated his imagination. No longer N.C., Ginsberg's marvelous boy, this was

Kerouac's Dean Moriarty, a man who burned in ecstasy and desperation. This Cassady had himself lost his "tenderest hopes." He had lost Ginsberg. He had tried writing but could produce nothing but trash. Then there was the coming child, whom he both wanted and feared. It was a figure in the pattern of his life to seek to be part of a family, to participate in the loving unit he never knew in childhood. Yet it was equally his motif, as it was his father's, to dismantle "families," to flee and to disappoint his loved ones at precisely the moment he felt the pressure of their expectation. Now, confronted with fatherhood and weighed down by assorted failures, he could not shake the feeling of "ennuied hysteria."

On February 8, 1948, Cassady celebrated his twenty-second birthday by sitting for fourteen hours in the backseat of a car, immersed in cold sweat and nausea, fighting for the nerve to put a silver revolver to his temple and pull the trigger. A month later he drove to Denver to get an annulment from LuAnne, knowingly making the trip through a blizzard without chains or antifreeze. Predictably, the automobile conked out in the Donner Pass, where the temperature was well below zero. He was saved from what was half-desired death, half-purgative descent into the void, when seven hours later the roadway was cleared behind him and a bus paused to disinter him.

By August 1948 he had emerged from despair. "Two weeks ago, if one can place a time on such things, I came out of the cauldron cleansed," he wrote. "I'm stronger, better in every way." True to form, he began a new regime of self-improvement fortified with his usual initial enthusiasm, although this time with a difference. He was changed, as Kerouac would presently observe.

That fall there was a rumor circulating in New York that Neal had commandeered a vehicle and was streaking east. Kerouac waited expectantly, but Cassady failed to show. Finally Jack decided to spend the Christmas holidays with his mother, "Mémère," and sister Nin at Nin's home in Kinston, North Carolina. A few days before Christmas, Kerouac heard a knock at the door and opened it to discover Neal and LuAnne dressed in white gas-station coveralls, bloodshot and grubby from a pell-mell trek that originated only days before in San Francisco. With them was Al Hinkle (Ed Dunkel in *On the Road*), Neal's adulating friend from Denver and fellow brakeman on the Southern Pacific.

Two events led to Neal's being in North Carolina. A November referendum on the railroad "full crew" law had been defeated, which meant that Neal's work hours were cut. More significantly, Neal had passed by an automobile showroom on Larkin Street, and had been assailed by a vision: a sleek maroon and silver '49 Hudson Hornet. Instantly, his regime of self-improvement took a back seat to a greater god. In thrall to the Hudson and all it portended, Neal offered up the family savings. Next he conned his buddy Al into marrying girl friend Helen (Galatea Dunkel in *On the Road*) earlier than planned, so she would join them in the trip east and, of course, spring for expenses. After several stormy discussions with Carolyn—who vowed, as she would so many times, not to take him back—Neal was off.

When Helen's money ran out, when she insisted upon adulterating the trip by stopping at motels, the Hinkle honeymoon came to an abrupt conclusion. The two road-crazed cads dumped her in Tucson and swung north for Denver. Neal was "too busy for scruples," too gone to worry about present wives. Indeed, he felt an atavistic yen for first wife LuAnne. The three of them—Al, Neal, LuAnne—consorted and roared east together, picking up a string of hitchhikers to make the gas money.

In Kinston, the sedate southern in-laws of Jack's sister Nin stared at the still-wired Cassady in hostile disbelief. Fortunately, Neal was so exhausted that all he wanted to do was *move*. Someone chanced to wonder aloud how a set of parlor furniture might be got to Ozone Park, New York, where Mémère, Jack's mother, lived and presto! Kerouac and Cassady had the tables and chairs stowed in the Hudson and were pushing north into their own element. It is at this point, one hundred pages deep in *On the Road*, that Kerouac's classic book truly begins. It is at this point that the "weird flower" that is Dean Moriarty is seen in full display.

"We've passed through all the forms," Cassady tells Kerouac in a calm moment during the return leg to Kinston. Neal recalls the days, seemingly long ago, when he was hot to glean from Nietzsche and Schopenhauer. "Everything since the Greeks has been predicated wrong. You can't make it with geometry and geometrical systems of thinking. It's all *this!*" he says, wrapping his finger in his fist, symbolizing both sexual and metaphysical union.

This is the post-ambitious Cassady, no longer "hincty" to demonstrate intellectual prowess, no longer anxious to figure in the world. Indeed, by 1949 Cassady is no longer traumatized by the vision he had in 1942 of degenerating into a sorry heap like his father or the dim company at The Metropolitan. "You see, man, you get older and troubles pile up," he says in *On the Road*. "Someday you and me'll be coming down an alley together at sundown and looking in the cans to see."

"You mean we'll end up old bums?" asks Kerouac.

"Why not, man? Of course we will if we want to, and all that. There's no harm ending that way. You spend a whole life of noninterference with the wishes of others, including politicians and the rich, and nobody bothers you and you cut along and make it your own way.... What's your road man?—holyboy road, madman road, rainbow road, guppy road, any road. It's an anywhere road for anybody anyhow."

Cassady as Dean Moriarty embodies what Paul Goodman thought the best impulse of the Beat movement: He is "resigned but searching." He is, in an earlier poet's words, intent upon "winning" by yielding to the tide.

He is, as well, newly and quirkily religious. "And no one can now tell us that there is no God," he says with the authority of one who has been to hell and returned. "Troubles, you see, is the generalization word for what God exists in. The thing is not to get hung-up."

Noting, out the window of the Hudson, a little kid
throwing stones at the cars on the highway, Cassady says,
"Think of it.... One day he'll put a stone through a
man's windshield and the man will crash and die—all on
account of that little kid. You see what I mean? God
exists without qualms. As we roll this way I am positive
beyond doubt that everything will be taken care of for
us...."
        This is not to say that Neal had mellowed.
Hardly. He had merely amplified his register. He'd de-
fined a new polarity, one that afforded a kind of
psychological safety net for the *salto mortale*: "God exists
without qualms.... everything will be taken care of for
us." Far from slowing down, Cassady's "every muscle
twitched to live and go." He seemed to be doing everything at once: shaking his head up and down, sideways,
in every direction; making complex structures in the air
with his hands; walking, sitting, standing, sitting again,
crossing and uncrossing his legs, getting up, rubbing his
hands, massaging his belly, patting his fly, hiking his
pants; all the while shifting in and out of a range of
W. C. Fields and Groucho Marx voices and poking and
tickling Kerouac and everyone else, and jabbering, jabbering, jabbering. His every act was at once a creation of
chaos and an intricate imposition upon it—whether he
was marshalling his troops for a gratuitous forced march
into tiny Kinston center ("There was no purpose in our
coming downtown, but he found purposes") or scrambling, then rearranging, the seating in the Hudson
("Marylou, honeythighs, you sit next to me, Sal next, then

Ed at the window..."). Cassady, wrote John Clellon
Holmes in a piece of understatement, "somehow usurped
the hostly function wherever he went."

"You only live once and eternally," Ginsberg
would later say. And Cassady knew this, always knew
this, but especially in the late forties when he jettisoned
conventional ideas of "making it." It was then that he
dedicated himself to the search for a different kind of
"it": to the search for what he called IT. IT was all about
time. IT was about damming up time or turning its flow
to torrent, about dislocating oneself into Meaning. In
effect, IT was about recapturing the "ebulliency" Cassady
first experienced at age seven when half brother Jimmy
buried him in the wall, a state of exhilaration that could
be induced in any number of ways: through sex and jazz
and drugs; above all, by going on the road.

"[On the Road's] importance," allowed the Beats' favorite
antagonist, Time magazine, "lies in author Kerouac's
attempt to create a rationale for the fevered young who
twitch around the nation's jukeboxes and brawl point-
lessly in the midnight streets." This is true enough, in
part. On the Road was decidedly of its moment. Everyone in 1957, everyone of a certain veteran age, that is,
knew what it was about even without opening its covers:
the latest juvenile heresy. It was the book the age demanded, then did not really need to read.

For the young, who read it, especially for young
males, On the Road was something more than an apol-
ogy for hipsterism. They felt in their marrow what was

classically American in Kerouac's book. Indeed, persons as diverse (and notable today) as politician Tom Hayden, singer Bob Dylan, novelist Thomas McGuane, and actor Nick Nolte have testified to the book's force as revelation. "I first read *On the Road* in high school in Omaha," said Nick Nolte, who might have been speaking for a generation in a recent interview. "I remember thinking, 'You mean you can do that? Pick up and go?' It seemed incredible to me."

Like so many American tales, *On the Road* is about escape, about lighting out for the perpetually receding territory ahead. True to classic American form, *On the Road* exists less as a novel than as a romance or poem—less, that is, as a complex net of relations than as a sequence of radiant images. The half dozen trips in the book resolve into cameos of freedom, snapshots of adolescent desire. Take, for example, the image of Jack and Neal and LuAnne driving naked across Texas wastes, of LuAnne brazenly applying cold cream and attentions to their respective parts, of a line of trucks visible in the rearview mirror swerving off the highway in amazement. Or the image of the same troika laboring through the night toward Mojave and reaching the Tehachapi Pass at dawn, of Neal switching off the gas and of the automobile careering thirty miles down the mountainside past other vehicles, through hairpin curves, and by low stone walls overlooking what seems the bottom of the world. Or the image of Neal and Jack in an Okie roadhouse in the Colorado hills, of Neal dashing madly into Denver and filching car after car, only to return and discard them at the roadhouse literally beneath the gaze of the police, who mill redundantly in the parking lot saying, "Somebody's been stealing cars left and right here!" Or the image of Neal and Jack as hitchhikers, exchanging the stories of their lives in the backseat of a ride, of the two of them so rapt in the rhythms of IT that they cause the vehicle to rock from side to side....

Yet *On the Road* is more than a series of compelling images. One might say—using language D. H. Lawrence applied to Fenimore Cooper's Leather Stocking Tales—that Kerouac's book works out the recurrent American dream of establishing "the nucleus of a new society." It is about the forging of a community of two, of an alternative world—alternative to the leaden adult world where needs are obstructed and pleasures of the flesh and spirit are bound and blunted.

Kerouac's peculiar achievement, or luck, was to hit upon the indelible emblem for his world apart. His vehicle was, of course, a vehicle: the automobile. It is possible to talk of the very action and shape of *On the Road* in terms of automobiles, e.g., "this was the episode of the '49 Hudson ... that of the 'fag Plymouth' ... that of the Cadillac limo ... and that of the '37 Ford." The automobile is Kerouac's equivalent to Melville's *Pequod* or Mark Twain's raft. Indeed, one might speak, as critics do of Mark Twain's raft, of the afflated values within Kerouac's vehicle and the "pedestrian" values without. It could be said that *On the Road* is the apotheosis of the automobile, a peculiarly American reconciliation of technology and romantic vision, the harnessing of the dread Twentieth Century Machine in the interest of the New World Garden.

"*On the Road* was good prose. I wasn't worried about the prose," said the redoubtable Malcolm Cowley, who finally convinced the Viking Press to publish Kerouac's book in 1957. "It seemed to me that in the original draft the story kept swinging back and forth across the continental United States like a pendulum. And one thing I kept putting forward to Jack was, 'Why don't you consolidate some of these episodes so that your hero doesn't swing across the country quite so often and so that the book has more movement.'"

Cowley was, of course, concerned to sell *On the Road* to the Viking editorial board, to make it readable. Yet his suggestion for giving the book more movement—*linear* movement—works against its special charm and reason for being. "What is the meaning of this voyage to New York?" the Kerouac and Cassady characters are asked near the middle of the volume. They stare dumbly at one another. "We sat and didn't know what to say; there was nothing to talk about anymore. The only thing to do was go." The only thing to do was to swing back and forth across the continent "like a pendulum" and thereby, in the space between upswing and downswing, *to describe a world*—a world apart sustained by endless kicks and digging-out-the-window and headlong conversation in which one rehearsed and reinvented the story of his life; a world furious with activity and movement but untainted by notions of progress or motive; a world not out of time so much as centered in the eye of time's pendulum.

On the Road is undeniably in the American grain. Like classic American tales ranging from *The Deerslayer* to *Red River*, it takes as its subject—again to quote D. H. Lawrence on Cooper—"a stark stripped human relationship of two men, deeper than the deeps of sex. Deeper than property, deeper than fatherhood, deeper than marriage, deeper than love." There are, of course, women in *On the Road*, but they are little more than apparatus. They serve only to provide occasions for contracting IT, for galvanizing a union "deeper than the deeps of sex." To plumb the depths of the Kerouac-Cassady relationship, as well as to understand its appeal for countless young people since 1957, it helps to know something about Kerouac's early life. For Kerouac is the man with recognizable human parts with whom one identifies, while Cassady is an interloper from another realm, a scandalous event looking for a place to happen.

Jack Kerouac had a seemingly conventional boyhood. Born in 1922, a few years before Cassady, he was the third child of Leo and Gabrielle (Mémêre) Kerouac, French Canadians living in Lowell, Massachusetts, where Leo ran a print shop. Leo was big, powerful, a "man's man" in the limited sense of the phrase: He was anti-intellectual, bigoted, reactionary, passionate about sports. He and Jack rarely communicated.

Dying of stomach cancer in 1946, shortly before
Kerouac met Cassady, Leo requested that Jack (called *Ti
Jean*) look after Mémère—a largely formal request, since
she always took care of Jack. She handled his finances
and—depending on how one sees it—either gave him the
emotional purchase that enabled his itinerancy, or en-
cumbered him with an attachment that prevented his
ever becoming fully adult. Most of Jack's friends, notably
his three wives, thought the relationship unnatural.

A Roman Catholic growing up in puritan New
England, Kerouac was visited—as if in accord with such
schema—with a double portion of guilt and sensitivity to
sin. No doubt he could have borne this double portion
with composure had it not been trebled through his
brother Gerard. Four years older than Jack, Gerard died
slowly at age nine of rheumatic fever. At first the
suffering was beautiful, conferring a spiritual luminosity
sometimes associated with tuberculosis. At the end the
choking and screaming were horrible.

Gerard's impact on Kerouac was critical. He was
generally regarded by the community as a saint, a sort of
toddling Francis of Assisi who held for the sacredness of
all living things. Gerard died and Ti Jean lived—that was
Kerouac's burden. Dead, Gerard would not keep still, but
haunted his younger brother and beckoned enigmatically:
"In darkness in mid-sleep night I saw him standing over
my crib with wild hair, my heart stoned," Kerouac wrote
in *Doctor Sax*. "I turned horrified, my mother and sister
were sleeping in big bed, I was in crib, implacable stood

Gerard-O my brother.... it might have been the arrangement of the shadows. —Ah Shadow! Sax!"

Young Kerouac was not entirely given over to
visions and metaphysical anguish. He was an athlete; he
was a fledgling writer, scribbling in his diary and con-
tributing sports pieces to the Lowell *Sun*. He was, too, a
voracious consumer of pop culture, of whatever could be
joyously drunk in at the movies and through the radio
and funnies. Above all, Kerouac adored Lamont Cranston,
"The Shadow": "I was in crib, implacable stood Gerard-O
my brother.... it might have been the arrangement of the
shadows. —Ah Shadow! Sax!"

For young Jack, Gerard-O and The Shadow
merged into an imaginary boyhood companion named
Doctor Sax. Protean, often invisible, Doctor Sax generally
dressed in a cape and slouch hat and wore a malevolent
leer. Like The Shadow, he was a cool customer whose
interior heat was betrayed by a maniacal laugh that
sprang forth without warning, a roaring "mwee hee hee
ha ha ha ha" of "inside secret sureness in the black." In
spite of his disturbing garb and laugh, which alienated
all but Ti Jean, Doctor Sax was a covert worker in "the
void," protecting people "from horrors they can never
know." Gerard would have understood and applauded his
mission; indeed, Sax was a crazed Gerard returned from
the void and trading exclusively in parables. Said young
Jack, "I know that Doctor Sax is speaking to the bottom
of my boy problems and they could all be solved if I
could fathom his speech."

Seen from a distance, Kerouac's life takes shape as a search for the knowing but shrouded brother. During the Beat years Jack would virtually apprentice himself to one new friend after another, to Lucien Carr, William Burroughs, Herbert Huncke, Gary Snyder. He seemed to regard each as, in some partial way, an avatar of Gerard/Sax.

About Cassady, he was less equivocal. In *On the Road,* we learn that Cassady as Dean Moriarty had a laugh like that of The Shadow or Sax: "His laugh was maniacal; it started low and ended high, exactly like that of a radio maniac." We learn, too, that he spoke elliptically: "There was nothing clear about what he said, but what he meant to say was somehow made pure and clear." What is more, "the sight of his suffering bony face ... and his straining muscular sweating neck made me remember my boyhood." And finally, "In spite of our differences in character, he reminded me of some long-lost brother." Kerouac should better have written, "*Because* of our differences in character, he reminded me of some long-lost brother."

One need only look at the photographs of Kerouac and Cassady during the Beat period to see how closely, at times, the two friends resembled one another. The likeness is especially provocative since Kerouac was black-haired and dark, while Cassady was lighter-haired and fair. It is a wry flick of significance, an ironic transposition of color symbolism, for Kerouac was the timid and virgin soul, while Cassady was the man of experience, the

man of "inside secret sureness in the dark." He was
Doctor Sax in the flesh, the enigmatic brother-as-Other.

As John Clellon Holmes has remarked, Jack Kerouac was "a deeply traditional nature thrown out of
kilter." Beat fringe character Locke McCorkle has said that
Kerouac "was the only person of that whole group who
my wife would trust to baby-sit the children." He was,
according to most accounts, not a passionate but an
affectionate lover; indeed, at one point in *On the Road* he
steps out of the frame to mourn the disappearance of
courtship from American life. He was diffident, self-
effacing, considerate to a fault. Neal and Carolyn specu-
lated, when Jack was living with them in 1952, that he
chose to urinate out his second-floor window rather than
chance seeing them nude on his way to the bathroom. He
preferred Muscatel or Tokay wine to marijuana and,
supreme irony, he was terrified of driving and hated
hitchhiking. In short, the King of the Beats was decidedly
unhip.

During the summer of 1949, while Cassady was
living in San Francisco with Carolyn and baby Cathy,
Kerouac and Mémêre moved to Westwood, Colorado, the
hills just outside Denver. Jack moved there in order to
recreate and inhabit his "brother's" life. He took a job
Neal once held in the wholesale fruit market in downtown Denver. During the evenings he wandered around
the city, taking special note of such storied haunts as The
Metropolitan and Peterson's pool hall. In a controversial
passage in *On the Road*, which James Baldwin found
condescending and Eldridge Cleaver admired, Kerouac
spoke of walking through the Denver "colored section"

Seated before The Snowdon in 1932, six-year-old Neal and half brother Jimmy. *(Courtesy of Carolyn Cassady)*

Neal Cassady in 1948, posing for Merchant Marine application.
*(Courtesy of Carolyn Cassady)*

LuAnne Henderson married Neal in 1945 when she was fifteen and he nineteen. *(Courtesy of Carolyn Cassady)*

Allen Ginsberg (right) and Paul Goodman at the Living Theater during the fifties. *(Photo ©1979 by Fred W. McDarrah)*

Neal with blood-brother Jack Kerouac in early fifties.
*(Courtesy of Carolyn Cassady)*

The legendary driver at the wheel of "Detroit iron."
*(Courtesy of Carolyn Cassady)*

"A rather typical illustration of
our relationship—especially in
the open," said Carolyn of this
photo. *(Photo by Jack Kerouac,
Courtesy of Carolyn Cassady)*

Neal with Diana Hansen, whom he married in 1950, and her family, in Tarrytown, N.Y. *(Courtesy of Carolyn Cassady)*

Carolyn in the summer of 1958, shortly after Neal was sent to San Quentin.
*(Courtesy of Carolyn Cassady)*

Jack Kerouac in the wake of *On the Road*—ravaged by the "bitch-goddess," Success.
*(Photo © by Fred W. McDarrah)*

Neal and Allen in 1963. *(Photo by Charles Plymell, Courtesy of City Lights)*

Shaving at Ginsberg's San Francisco apartment in early sixties.
*(Photo ©1965 by Larry Keenan, Jr.)*

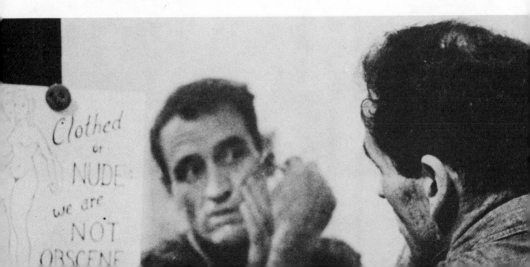

The Beat Generation's "last gathering," 1965, in front of the City Lights Book Store. (Photo ©1968 by Larry Keenan, Jr.)

Ken Kesey in 1966: "I saw that Cassady did everything a novel does, except that he did it better because he was living it and not writing about it."
*(Photo ©1967 by Larry Keenan, Jr.)*

"Furthur," the Merry Prankster bus. *(Photo ©1966 by Ted Streshinsky)*

Mountain Girl
with her baby Sunshine.
*(Photo ©1966 by Ted Streshinsk)*

**Jerry Garcia, leader of
The Grateful Dead.**
*(Photo ©1980 by Herbie Greene)*

Cassady the sidereal
and sure-handed hammer flipper.
(Photo ©1966 by Ted Streshinsky)

Wavy Gravy, onetime protégé
of Lenny Bruce and head
of the Hog Farm commune.
*(Photo by Carol Scott)*

Neal and Ann Murphy—their
relationship recalled the John
Wayne-Maureen O'Hara
donnybrook in *The Quiet Man*.
*(Photo ©1966 by Larry Keenan, Jr.)*

Kesey rapping at an Acid Test
(one of a dozen LSD-fueled
multimedia fetes held along
the West Coast in 1965
and 1966).
*(Photo ©1966 by Ted Streshinsky)*

Neal as countercultural celebrity and focus of admiration.
*(Photo ©1966 by Ted Streshinsky)*

Telepathic communion with the Merry Pranksters.
*(Photo ©1966 by Ted Streshinsky)*

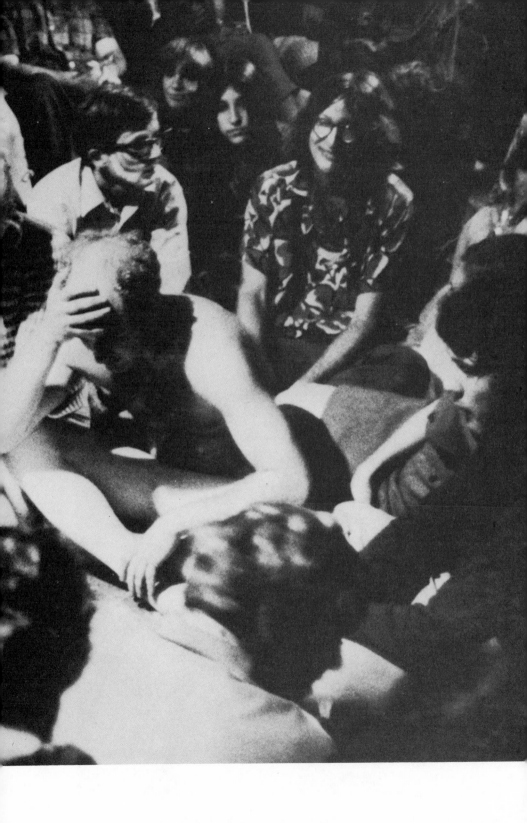

Early summer 1967 in San Miguel de Allende, Mexico—one of the last snapshots of Neal. *(Courtesy of Carolyn Cassady.)*

and wishing he were a Negro, "feeling that the best the white world had offered was not enough ecstasy … not enough life, joy, kicks, darkness, music, not enough night." He wished he were a Denver Mexican "or even a poor overworked Jap"—anything but what he was: a disillusioned white man with white ambitions. Naturally, the derelict neighborhoods and Negro streets merged in his mind with Cassady, the fair-complexioned but "dusky" brother, the spirit of the alien place.

In his extraordinary homage to Neal, *Visions of Cody*, Jack refers to him as both his "lover" and his "enemy." He sees him as "an angel, a god," but also as "a devil" and "an old witch." Cassady is a host of welded opposites. He is at times a sort of *madeleine* or cake to dip into the solution of the past to retrieve comforting images of a prewar world in which everyone was fresh-faced and forthcoming. But he is also the Shrouded Stranger who lurked in the shadows of Kerouac's child-hood threatening death. Sometimes Neal is John Doe, the average "fellow who works for a living and has a wife and kids and worries about Taxes in March." Yet he is also proper metal for heroic castings by Robert Burns and Thomas Carlyle: His waist is thinner and his arms bigger than Brando's in *Streetcar*, he can "blow" with Bird and Diz and Slim, and he can tame lions with the verve of Clyde Beatty. He is the Green Hornet in a world of Bartlebys and Pulham Esquires. But he is also Jesus scourged and crucified.

"I once saw Neal look at Jack," John Clellon Holmes would recall, "and I imagined I saw in Neal's face, 'You're not seeing me anymore.'" Indeed, Jack was seeing, at least when seated before a blank sheet of typing paper, a good deal more than Neal *qua* Neal. He was seeing his personal Rosetta stone, the key to the high and low languages of his being. In Kerouac's mind, Cassady grew from being Gerard *redux* to being the incarnation of the "Fellaheen" or alien Third World, to being something as hulkingly significant and elusively multivalent as Moby Dick: in several parts, a bittersweet myth of Lost America, a titillating fantasy of super power, a seriocomic tall tale. It is no mere rhetorical flourish to say that Jack was possessed by Neal. He was, in Melville's word, utterly "heaped" by him.

Needless to say, perhaps, not everyone was as enchanted with Neal. Even the Beats divided on his charm. Both Burroughs and Ginsberg disapproved of his helter-skelter. Ginsberg spoke of the "pathos" of Neal's life: that he was "doomed never to rise out of time and illusion." Burroughs made the case against him with severity: "He is the mover, compulsive, dedicated, ready to sacrifice family, friends, even his car itself to the necessity of moving from one place to another. Wife and child may starve, friends exist only to exploit for gas money. Neal must move." (It should be said that Cassady did not always number among Burroughs's fans either, remarking that Burroughs "was as high-horse as a Governor in the Colonies, as nasty as an old Aunt, and as queer as the day is long.")

The case against Cassady is made, however, with fullest authority—and for all the straight, un-Beat world—by the Helen Hinkle character in one of the more memorable scenes in *On the Road*. It is late in the summer of 1949. Kerouac has quit Denver and his project of reliving Neal's youth and has caught a bus to San Francisco. He goes immediately to the Cassady house on Russian Hill. Neal answers the door, per usual, in the nude. Knowing instinctively what is in the offing—kicks, her desertion—Carolyn greets Jack with a scowl, then builds to a fit of anger and tears. The Cassady household is in bad repair: The Hudson has been repossessed, a second child is accidentally on the way, Neal has broken his thumb on LuAnne's skull and has developed osteomyelitis. Even as Carolyn is ejecting the Beat duo from her house, Kerouac notices a large oil painting of Helen Hinkle hanging in the living room over the sofa. Instantly he realizes that the two women have been spending lonely months together commiserating over the cruel madness of their men.

In search of accommodations for the night, Neal and Jack end up at the Hinkles' place. Al is off on the road himself, however, with Jim Holmes, the billiards virtuoso of Neal's youth. The two of them are reportedly bent for Portland, Maine. Naturally, no one knows just why. That night, amid other friends convened from Denver, Helen Hinkle, as Galatea Dunkel in Kerouac's book, enjoys a modicum of revenge. "All you think about," she lights into Neal, "is what's hanging between your legs and how much money or fun you can get out of people and then you just throw them aside. Not only that but you're silly about it. It never occurs to you that life is serious and there are people trying to make something decent out of it instead of just goofing all the time."

Kerouac starts to come to Cassady's defense, but he is disarmed by epiphany, by the truth posed obliquely in Helen Hinkle's words. He looks over at Cassady, who is typically oblivious of the world's opinion of him, who is in his own realm, sweating, veins popping, chanting, "Yes, yes, yes" quietly to himself. That's what Neal is, Kerouac realizes. *The Holy Goof!*

"I didn't want to interfere, I just wanted to follow," Kerouac says at one point. And at another: "Somewhere along the line I knew there'd be girls, visions everything; somewhere along the line the pearl would be handed to me."

That would be Mexico in the summer of 1950. It was the trip for which all previous trips were but anticipatory shadows. The excursion to Mexico is special because it is the longest, because it is the most ecstatic and raw, because it is Kerouac and Cassady's last road adventure. It has a dual quality of elegy. The two men are launched by Neal's old Denver gang—they rise to the send-off, then settle back wistfully into their roles as "responsible adults." Secondly, Neal and Jack draft a third party for the expedition, a kid named Frank Sheperd who yells "Sonof-a*bitch*! Hot *damn*!" in quenchless enthusiasm at every turn of the highway. There is a sense in this final episode that "road knowledge," a *modus vivendi*, is being passed on by two wily, if still wide-eyed veterans to a new generation.

The trip begins as a primer. Passing Pikes Peak, heading down the Pueblo highway, they decide to tell the stories of their lives, one by one. Frank is to start. "We've got a long way to go," counsels Neal, "so you must take every indulgence and deal with every single detail you can bring to mind—and still it won't all be told." Soon they are out of Colorado, through New Mexico, and into Texas. All the while Neal brings Frank out, coaches him through his history, extrapolating, adding, savoring. In Texas, from Amarillo to Childress, Neal and Jack take over and regale Frank with plot upon plot of books they've read, giving him context against which to play his own story.

In San Antonio, Neal offers crucial lessons in *digging*: "Dig, now, out of the corner of your eye and as we listen to Wyonie [Blues Harris] blow about his baby's pudding and as we smell the soft air as you say—dig the kid, the crippled kid shooting pool at one table, the butt of the joint's jokes, y'see, he's been the butt all his life. The other fellows are merciless but they love him." *Digging*, Frank would learn, is the unspeakable vision of the individual: the visceral intuition of ineffable harmonies. It partakes of what Cassady would elsewhere call the "gloat of knowledge": "Looking out anxiously on the whole of all that's before me each moment as tho I was about to die every minute and therefore straining all ways to *feel* the experience fully and hunger to store it all and save everything in the mind so that when I feel any similar emotion it will recall the scene and conversely, when I see any object or hear any sound that has the aspects of an object or sound that was seen or heard in one of the moments when I gathered in a strong emotion, I can then, whenever it's necessary, release some of the hoarded memory to think of it and when I do the resultant emotion becomes one of gloat...."

Soon there is Mexico. It's only the sleazy border town Nuevo Laredo, but it looks like "holy Lhasa." Perceived with washed eyes and blinkered concentration, the landscape presents itself in miraculous parcels. As Sabinas, Monterrey, Montemorelos flick by, so do the recognitions: That the houses of the *peones* have no doors, that you can peer into their material lives, *that there is no suspicion in Mexico.* That men and women, boys and girls, go about exclusively in groups, *that nobody's ever alone in Mexico.* That these people sweat the year round, that their sweat is heavy, sluggish like fine olive oil, *that Mexicans know nothing of nonsweat and therefore must be different in their very souls.* That these are not the insipid Pedros and Panchos of cheapjack American lore, that they have high cheekbones and slanted eyes and soft ways, *that they are Indians, the grave fathers of mankind.*

It is in Gregoria that Neal, Jack, and Frank come into "girls, visions, everything." They happen onto a young Mexican with sad eyes named Victor, who in turn supplies them with marijuana, a ponderous stogie of tea: "To drag on the thing was like leaning over a chimney and inhaling.... The sweat froze on our foreheads and it was suddenly like the beach at Acapulco." Barriers of race and language fall. Without knowing a word of Spanish, the preternaturally intuitive Cassady clearly understands all that Victor and his clustering friends are saying. "Yes, of course!" says Cassady as Dean Moriarty in *On the Road*. "There's not a doubt in my mind! Decidedly, man! Oh, indeed! Why, pish, posh, you say the dearest things to me!" Kerouac sees a nimbus prickling around Cassady's figure: "He looks like God."

Arm in arm with the visions come the girls. Victor takes them to a stucco whorehouse equipped with a jukebox that screams mambo and marimba by Pérez Prado. The girls are more than willing, they are ravenous for men and dancing and drink. Frank pairs up with a fifteen-year-old with almond-colored skin and a dress buttoned halfway up and halfway down. Predictably, Neal latches onto the wild woman in the brothel, a Venezuelan in a flimsy housecoat who is part Indian, part white. Equally predictable, Jack is chased down by a fat and boorish slut with a small dog, even as he aches for a dark and wispy teenager whom he instantly loves and therefore will not touch. "It was like a long, spectral Arabian dream in the afternoon of another life...."

Hours and thirty-six American dollars later, they tear themselves away, in spite of the objections of Frank, who wants to start all over again—who is, in fact, beginning to out-Moriarty Moriarty. Once more on the road to Mexico City, they discover that their headlights are gone and that their vision is further impaired by a cloud of insects. They debate going back to Gregoria, but receive new impetus from Frank, who is bonkers in the backseat, yelling "Hot *damn!*" "He's so high," says Neal, admiringly, "he knows what he's doing!" They ride on, plunge into the blackness. The insects scream, the smell gets ranker, the jungle thickens. In best Cassady fashion, they take off their T-shirts and surrender themselves to chance and the dark.

They stop to sleep near Limón, and an extraordinary thing happens to Kerouac. Hopelessly uncomfortable in the pool of his sweat in the car, he decides to stretch out on the roof. There is no breeze, and myriad dead bugs clot in cakes on his skin, but he comes to the sudden realization that "the jungle takes you over and you become it. Lying on top of the car with my face to the black sky was like lying in a closed trunk on a summer night. For the first time in my life the weather was not something that touched me, that caressed me, froze or sweated me, but became me. The atmosphere and I became the same."

Sinking into the jungle night, Kerouac lapses into a version of the "amazed somnolency" that Cassady himself first experienced in the Pride of the Rockies flour mill. A man appears by the car and flashes a light. "*Dormiendo?*" he asks gently, indicating Neal supine in the road. Yes, says Jack, he's sleeping. And the spectral sheriff trundles off. Then just before dawn, the hour of waking dream, Kerouac hears dogs barking and the sound of hooves. He sees an apparition: A wild sheet-white horse trots down the road directly toward Neal.

Kerouac feels no panic. The horse sees Neal and passes right by his head, much as a ghostly ship. It whinnies softly and continues into town, then back into the jungle on the other side.

The jungle had spoken—in parable, of course. The abyss had rendered up a "pearl." But there would be a further price for "ebulliency" demanded of Kerouac in the world of experience. Neal and Jack would reach Mexico City, which they would dig like crazy, but Jack would fall delirious with dysentery. Worse still, Neal would desert him, leave him cold and sweating in his sickbed. The nonmythic Cassady would rear his rapacious and pathetic head. "He had a devil-may-care attitude," Herbert Huncke would say of Neal. "[But] he was a very nervous, worried cat all the time." Indeed, at this junction he had reason to worry. He was about to become married to two women at once.

PART THREE

THE
GOOD
BOURGEOIS

*He [Neal] is already on top of the world.*
*What to do with world is next problem.*

ALLEN GINSBERG in a letter to
Carolyn Cassady, late 1952

Supposedly, Neal went to Mexico to get a quick divorce
from Carolyn. He never quite got around to it. No matter,
leaving Jack to the care of Bill and Joan Burroughs, who
were living in Mexico City, he pushed the '37 Ford
stateside until its engine dropped out in Lake Charles,
Louisiana. He then took a plane to New York, where on
July 10, 1950, he committed bigamy with an unwitting
and pregnant Diana Hansen.

She was a tall, dark-haired woman with, according to Kerouac, the air of a Parisian coquette. From a
genteel Tarrytown, New York, family, she worked as a
model and was married to a poet when Neal met her.
Kerouac had introduced them at a party in Manhattan in
the fall of 1949, and John Clellon Holmes was there to
witness the encounter, which was vintage Cassady. "I saw
him score," Holmes recalled in *Jack's Book*. Neal simply
walked in, stunned her with a glance, and moved into
her apartment. "She was completely New York literary
establishment," said Holmes, "and she'd never seen anything like Neal, who came roaring into her life."

During the fall and winter months of 1949–50
Holmes often visited the couple at Diana's place in the

East Eighties. "I remember going up there. The shades were always drawn, and they had a red light, or something. Neal wore a short kimono with his dork showing underneath it—just the tip. And here was Diana—how do I say this without sounding sexist?—all she wanted was for him to love her and she was willing for anything."

Kerouac, meanwhile, was busy that winter with an early draft of *On the Road* and was an infrequent visitor to Neal's New York love nest. He saw enough, however, to recognize that Cassady, when out of bed, was occupying himself—taking in jazz, performing tricks with his deck of pornographic cards, working the parking lots—much as he had been on the other side of the continent with Carolyn.

Something like this recognition must have occurred, over time, to Cassady as well. For after deserting Kerouac and returning from Mexico in the summer of 1950—indeed, two hours after "marrying" Diana—he used his brakeman's pass to board a train to San Francisco. Ostensibly he was returning to the coast to keep his seniority with the Southern Pacific, but upon arrival he promptly asked Carolyn to take him back and was furious to discover she was seeing another man. He moved to Watsonville, the end of his freight run. He made the move purportedly to enable Diana to come out and to do Carolyn a service by keeping Diana out of her sphere of activity. His emerging motive was, however, to design a triangle of wives past and present. The ubiq-

uitous LuAnne had also been summoned to Watsonville
and was working at a drive-in.

The arrangement was never actually brought off.
LuAnne rebelled against Neal's possessiveness (he spent
entire nights in a telephone booth watching the drive-in)
and left town. Eventually Diana made contact with
Carolyn and tore the tissue of stratagems meant to keep
the women apart and docile. Heavy with the son she
would deliver in November, Diana flew back to New
York, and Neal moved in with Carolyn and their two
daughters, Cathy and Jami, the latter having been born
while Neal was wintering in Manhattan. "I had to let
him stay," said Carolyn, who was seriously in need of
financial and familial support. And stay he would for
more than a decade.

Carolyn Cassady, née Robinson, was the daughter of a
professor, the head of biochemistry at the Vanderbilt
Medical School in Tennessee. Growing up on a refur-
bished plantation twenty-two miles outside Nashville, she
passed an apparently idyllic childhood. She knew nothing
of the Depression. Of the greater world she knew only
that some vague unpleasantness in Europe was prevent-
ing her, at age fourteen in 1938, from emulating her
sister and going to school there.

Circumstances seemed to conspire to keep her
naive. She was the youngest of five children and was not
taken as seriously as she would have liked. She attended
only girls' schools from eighth grade through Bennington

College. She had few companions during the teen years, since the plantation was fairly isolated; thus she spent the better part of her extracurricular hours drawing and reading and riding her horse. In her solitude, she nurtured traditional romantic tastes. She would always, for example, prefer the Brontë sisters to Kerouac.

Her father was no ogre, just puritanic. He tolerated little display of affection, no touching at all; indeed, Carolyn never kissed him until he was sixty-five. His morality, which dominated the household, was dour, black and white with no shadings. Negative thinking was, in his mind, plain common sense. Sex was a low biological incident between barely consenting adults and was not to be discussed even in private. Carolyn was not instructed on menstruation, much less the mechanics of love.

In such an atmosphere, it was small wonder that her eldest brother at age seventeen frequently entered her bedroom nude and erect, and that a second brother and a friend plotted to swap their respective sisters in an episode that left all involved feeling dirty and guilty. Not the least affected was Carolyn: "I gained a healthy dislike for the male organ," she said. In spite of this dislike, she was burdened during her high school years with the reputation of being "easy"—this due, in part, to her platinum blonde hair, the badge of loose women, the tribe of Harlow, in the movies. Repeatedly, she was rejected by boys her age both for supposed promiscuity and for not delivering upon demand.

At age twenty she was unwillingly deflowered by a thirty-five-year old big-city radio singer whom she kept asking about a perpetually imminent divorce. During her early twenties, she was courted by a lieutenant commander in the Naval Reserve, a swell who offered a sometimes appealing jet-set life, but who was more impressive on paper than in the flesh. Then there was the city planner, an Englishman whom her anglophile parents eyed as ideal marriage stock. Carolyn vehemently disagreed.

Her only satisfactory sexual relation took place in the middle 1940s in Denver. There she met an older engineering student. She appreciated his soft-focus romanticism, his strict code of modesty, his "no kinks intercourse" with the lights out. She discovered that he had a more experienced and inventive lover on the side; in any case, with the coming of spring 1947, the engineering student dumped her for a still more pristine undergraduate. Shortly thereafter Carolyn was pursued by a young Denver man named Bill Tomson, who regaled her with wild adventures in which he generally figured as the principal. Little by little it became clear that the exploits were initiated not by Tomson but by his friend Neal Cassady.

Foolishly, Tomson brought Neal by Carolyn's room in the Colburn Hotel. It was Tomson's undoing, for he paled beside the authentic article. Neal's looks were "pretty medium," Carolyn thought. But his dress—pinstripe suit, white T-shirt, bare neck—and overall presence was compelling. He had a "Runyonesque flavor," he exuded a "dangerous glamour." There was more: He was obviously a person of intellectual stature. He allowed that he went to Columbia College with Hal Chase, Ed White, et al., and soon he would be seasoning his *film noir* appeal with poetry, romantic lyrics written by Ginsberg which he passed off to Carolyn as his own. It was as if the civilized Edgar Linton and the elemental Heathcliff had stepped from *Wuthering Heights* and merged into one rock-ribbed man.

About this time, Cassady wrote Ginsberg detailing Carolyn's attractions. "Her chief quality," he said, "lies in the same sort of awareness or intuitive sense of understanding which is ours." He admired her lack of cynicism and "artificial sophistication." He spoke of the feeling of tranquility she instilled in him when they were together. Yet she was not pliant to his purposes. "Her basic inhibitions," he said, "are subtle psychological ones tied up indirectly with conventions [manners] and taste." In sum, "she is just a bit too straight for my temperament; however, that is the challenge...."

Cassady took up the gauntlet the evening of their first meeting. At midnight, all were about to desert Carolyn's hotel room where an impromptu party had been struck; in the number were Tomson, Al Hinkle and date, Neal and wife LuAnne. As Cassady headed toward the elevator, he turned to Carolyn and mysteriously held up two fingers. At 2 A.M. he reappeared at her door, suitcase in hand. She could not simply dismiss him. She was the only single woman, the only boarder under age fifty in the hotel, and she was already on the outs with management. She could not so much as argue in the hallway without being compromised.

Having gained access to the room, Neal was now busy parlaying his way from couch to bed. He was assuring her that his marriage to LuAnne was over. (Yes, she thought, it seemed to be. Well, maybe.) He was talking about how silly it was to let half the double bed go fallow. It didn't make sense. (It didn't, when you put it the way he put it.) Carolyn was feeling increasingly sophomoric, and in a trice Neal was between the sheets.

His master tactic was, however, to fall asleep instantly and to leave her awake and vigilant the night through, admiring his backhanded chivalry. It was masterful, too, in the morning to further bemuse and win her by seeking no additional advantage—to spend the morning helping her fashion a delicate spiderweb for a miniature stage set for a course in theater design, to sit there in a chair disarmingly engrossed in stringing tiny glass beads on a fine wire with clumsy panatela-size fingers.

Charmed by Neal's aura of accomplishment and his tactical support of her delicacy, convinced of LuAnne's abdication as wife, and stimulated by a first go with Benzedrine, it is no wonder that three weeks later Carolyn suspended her dislike of the male organ and surrendered her citadel. Nor is it surprising, considering Neal's initiation in love beneath his father's gaze, that Carolyn was deeply disappointed in their first sex together. "He was a raging animal; this could only be lust, not love. Bewildered, angry, crushed, I braced myself against the onslaught, fighting back my tears and the threatening screams. How could he help but notice my sudden frigidity? I was half grateful, half sorry that he didn't...." She found to her horror, as sundry women had and would to their delight, that Neal never enjoyed sex without violence. "The only way he was not able to do it was when I was offering or willing," she would later say in an interview with *Rolling Stone* magazine. "It had to be rape. Until finally I only submitted because I was afraid of him. At last, then, I said, 'I can't stand it anymore, kill me or whatever,' and much to my surprise he was very nice about it, he seemed to understand." He would find his sex elsewhere, and up his quota of masturbation.

This was just the first blow in a decade of disappointments for Carolyn, which is not to say there were no compensations. Neal was, of course, wonderfully alive and intellectually stimulating. Singular among the Beats, he was a fairly good provider. He was an exemplary father. He was, perhaps, too good a father, as he often defeated Carolyn's attempts at discipline. By September 1951 there were three children: Cathy, Jami, and John Allen (named for Kerouac and Ginsberg). The marriage was sealed and Carolyn's "trial" scarcely begun; at least such is the sense one gets from reading her unpublished memoir (from which *Heart Beat* has been excerpted).

In a way, the memoir is more novelistic than *On the Road*. It calls to mind the first novels in English,

written by Samuel Richardson and his many imitators, in
which the chaste and staunchly bourgeois heroine is
tricked into situations where her virtue is compromised
by a latter-day Renaissance rake. Much as Richardson's
Clarissa, Carolyn endures a domestic drama in which
every glance, every gesture, every exchange is laden with
ambiguous significance. She spends much of her life with
Neal trying to read his behavior for signs of impending
catastrophe, trying to anticipate his scams or her desertion, trying to salvage her dignity and peace of mind. Her
memoir is, in sum, an alternately magnanimous and
peevish chronicle of a conventional woman's eccentric
growth, of Carolyn's mostly unsuccessful attempt to live
with an extraordinary man on his own outrageous terms.

Neal, for his part, did try to become more responsible
during the fifties. He took to Roman Catholic priests
what he himself came to credit as his "problem with
adjustment." He attended the Langley-Porter Clinic in San
Francisco, where he submitted, up to a point, to psycho-
analytic procedures: He played at free association and
deciphering ink blots, but he balked at fully surrendering
to the soul-swirl of analysis itself. He often attended
sessions high on tea.

Cassady's most striking response to the pressures
to "conform," and to his mounting guilt over his inability
to do so, was his lapse into what Kerouac diagnosed as
"blankness." At first Neal regarded this lapse with a
certain detachment. "I am listless without reason," he

wrote. "I sit as would Rodin's statue were his left arm dangling." Then, commensurate with the increasing need he felt to assume an adult role, he became alarmed, "I can't overemphasize too strongly how ugly my life has become, simply because of this 'do nothingness,' and how low I've gotten by realizing emotionally *every* damn moment what a really disgusting fish I am." He found that he could do neither the ordinary things, such as brushing his teeth, nor the necessary things, such as replacing the spark plugs in the car. "Suffice to say I just eat every 12 hours, sleep every 20 hours, masturbate every 8 hours and otherwise just sit on the train and stare ahead without a thought...." His psyche appeared to be intractable: It was as if the place where he most and best lived would no longer suffer itself to be colonized by regimes of "self-improvement."

Typically, Cassady experimented with his new-found context and peculiar chemistry. He attempted to transmute the "blankness" by plunging still further into it, by stepping up his consumption of marijuana. He had had an extraordinary experience in 1950, brought on by "bad green" or uncured marijuana. It was a trip that lasted several days. The first day he experienced the exhilaration of old: the eyelids pasted open, the buzzing in the head, polychromatic visions. The second day he flirted with omniscience. Everything he'd ever known or read or heard or thought returned in a flood and reassembled in a spectacular kaleidoscope of Meaning. He could do nothing but quiver with gratitude and awe, "Yes, yes, yes." The third day brought the tariff; there

was hell to pay. He underwent a series of waking
nightmares that bent him double and caused him to cry
out with such anguish that the neighbors came to his
assistance. Undaunted by the ordeal, he got in his car
and rushed to LuAnne and induced her to try the bad
tea. Her trip, as somehow he knew it would, duplicated
his own station by station and to the finest gradient. He
knew he loved her so much he had to kill her, but didn't.

Most of his life Cassady had had periods of
semiconsciousness, dozing stupors or moments of vividness in which he had "great impressions of things." In
the early forties, after reform school and while freshly
ambitious to cut a swath through the world, he had
drifted into waking dreams of himself as a great orator, a
sort of Patrick Henry of penal theory. In these reveries he
expounded notions of prison reform: He lectured grandly
on the use of psychiatrists and therapeutic apparatus, on
the disposition of convicts to the gallows or the asylum or
the whorehouse. He was as well, during the early forties,
bludgeoned by guilt and inferiority dreams that would
leave him unmanned for days. Later, when under the star
of Kerouac and Ginsberg, he attempted to put the mate-
rials of his visions to literary use. He spoke of writing a
play that combined tragedy and symbolic dance, Shakespeare and Martha Graham, and of composing the play
in the stream-of-consciousness style of James Joyce.

Later in the fifties, living in San Jose with
Carolyn, Neal grew six-foot marijuana plants in the
vacant lot beside his house. He made repeated forays into
San Francisco, fifty miles away, to cop an ounce or a joint

or just to fill his lungs with "weeded air." His every letter to everybody during this period included a request for grass: Did they have any? Would they send him some? By the fifties Cassady was not waiting to be overtaken by the "mystic spin." The days on the road with Kerouac a mere memory, he sought to find IT in marijuana. Redeeming his blankness through psychoactive drugs, he would create at least a facsimile of a "world apart," a species of divided self.

Neal was caught in a double bind. His choices were dire: loss of family and the only sustained love and support he had ever known, or loss of signature, his radical rootlessness and commitment to "ebulliency." The splitting of self was actually a strategy of conservation. It was an alternative to placing himself on Procrustes' bed and seeing his essential extremities lopped off in the interest of "fitting in." To quote R. D. Laing, one might say that Neal's schizophrenia was a "successful attempt *not* to adapt to pseudo-social realities."

Interestingly, while in the throes of worldly failure, Cassady came into his own as a writer. Even while complaining of "do nothingness" and mental vacancy, he wrote twenty- and thirty-page letters that astonished Kerouac and Ginsberg and convinced them that he was the one true writer among them. "Neal is a colossus risen to Destroy Denver!" said Kerouac upon reading the 23,000 word "Joan Anderson letter."

The legendary letter, which apparently survives only in part, begins with language appropriate to Cassady, the Hero of the Descent and the Return: "To have seen a specter isn't everything, and there are death-masks piled, one atop the other, clear to heaven. Commoner still are the wan visages of those returning from the shadow of the valley. This means little to those who have not lifted the veil." The letter proceeds to tell how Cassady lost one of the loves of his youth. She was a Jennifer Jones look-alike who aborted his child, and then, out of the hospital, pathetically waited and waited for Neal as he callously lushed with a friend at a nearby bar.

The story proper was the least of the letter's attractions. What entranced Kerouac especially was the virile rush and spew of the style. The letter was a concoction of tones and digressions, of asides, interpolated stories, and jokes which added up, in Kerouac's mind, to splendid spendthrift writing. What's more, there was method behind this inspired randomness. Neal advised Jack and Allen that the letter was the product of three Benzedrine-soaked afternoons and evenings, and that his way was to use the first word that came to him and not to alter a line laid down.

What followed is only too familiar to those acquainted with Beat lore. Early in April 1951, Jack Kerouac seated himself at the kitchen table of his Manhattan apartment and fed a massive roll of Chinese art paper through the cylinder of his typewriter. He was off and blistering his usual one hundred words a minute. Within a few pages he was writing, "the only people for me are the mad ones, the ones who are mad to live, mad to talk, mad to be saved, desirous of everything at the same time, the ones who never yawn or say a commonplace thing, but burn, burn, burn like fabulous yellow Roman candles...." With a Max Roach record providing percussive impetus, and with Cassady's "spontaneous style" as a release into "wild form," Kerouac raced through the 175,000 words of *On the Road* in just twenty days.

During the winter and spring of 1951, Neal himself had been writing. He'd been working up the autobiographical fragments that would be published in 1971 as *The First Third*. The seamless letters of the period are an index to the relative ease with which he was composing. He was even trying his hand at light verse:

> *So I long to lick the Lymph Gland larder*
> *of bubbly juices and harder tarter,*
> *And makee amends with a woman's Tits; and farter,*
> *and stick my neck in the noose of her garter,*
> *A plaything's above it to which I'm a martyr.*

Initially, the commotion that Kerouac and Ginsberg made over the Joan letter thrilled the "gurgles" out of him. He boasted that he could match that performance anytime, but ominously added, "not now tho." Success was beginning to catch up with him and to constrict his genius.

On May 15, 1951, he posted a letter to Ginsberg reporting that he had done no work on his manuscript in a month. He mentioned the difficulty of writing on a railroad schedule. Yet his real problem lay in a new and complicated relation to the act of writing. Suddenly he worried about grammar, faults in logic, shallowness, looseness and tightness of style. He worried, in effect, about all those matters that Kerouac, liberated by Cassady's earlier letters, had dismissed as academic.

Neal's most acute problem was with words themselves and with their curious power over him. He found that individual words insisted upon their use but would not aggregate to form a unit. As a result he was left with heavily overloaded sentences. He discovered himself switching words about as if they were boxcars and he a tyro brakeman long on zeal and short on savvy. Worse still, when by accident he hit the wrong key on the typewriter, he felt compelled not to erase. He felt obliged to canvass his mind for a new word for the mistaken letter to start. In thrall to the errant play of his fingers on the keyboard, he was soon burdened with a quantity of miscellaneous and imperial words that stared back at him like dopey runes. The issue of this problem was that he ceased writing *The First Third.* Soon he would even stop writing letters. The false spring past, he descended still deeper into blankness.

During 1951, however, he did muster a number of letters crafted to entice Kerouac to his small house at 29 Russell Street on the wrong side of San Francisco's fashionable Russian Hill. He offered Kerouac the attic, an ascetic work space conducive to great hermetic labor, even as he promoted the rest of the house and its resources as a pleasure dome suitable to Kubla Khan. All would be gratis, Neal would get him a railroad job, plus Carolyn was anxious to consider the past past and make friends. The letters were more than Kerouac could bear. He arrived in San Francisco in January 1952.

Carolyn found Jack a thoughtful if somewhat unsettling guest, who shared intimate details almost from the start. He discussed his troubles with his second wife, Joan Haverty, who had been the girl friend of Bill Cannastra. They had married impulsively shortly after Cannastra met his grisly end in the subway late in 1950. "I caught her with this Puerto Rican a couple of times," said Jack, "and now she's pregnant and says it's my child.... HA ... it ain't my child." Carolyn wondered at his judgment in women but was pleased that he took so to her own little girls, Cathy and Jami, who caused him only delight. Babies were another matter, however, and Jack gave namesake John Allen a generous berth.

Neal got Jack work in the baggage room of the railroad depot, since brakeman duty was in short supply. Soon, however, both men were home for extended periods as the railroad entered a lull, and soon Carolyn's old anxieties returned. Increasingly the two men sealed themselves off in Jack's attic or marched gaily out the door in search of kicks, leaving Carolyn to feel herself a "neglected household drudge."

On Neal's twenty-sixth birthday, February 8, 1952, Carolyn awoke sensing numbness on the side of her face. A doctor advised that she had Bell's palsy, a temporary paralysis apparently brought on by emotional strain. She was forced to wear an eye patch since the eye did not close, and to attach a paper clip to a rubber band and hook her mouth to her ear since her mouth would not otherwise remain in place. The grotesqueness of her appearance, in tandem with her pique following Kerouac's one-night spiriting a young black woman to the attic, led Jack and Neal to feel remorse and be more considerate. Carolyn would undergo six months of physical therapy, however, before the palsy completely subsided.

One evening Neal reported that the railroad was sending him to San Luis for a two-week local hold-down. As he was leaving he turned to Jack and Carolyn, still seated at the dinner table, and said, "Well, you know what they say ... 'My best pal and my best gal.'" Then he was gone, leaving his best pal and gal fumbling profitlessly in embarrassment.

When Neal returned, Carolyn expressed her hurt, then asked whether he had been making a serious suggestion or just trying to cover himself against what might happen. "A little of both, I suppose," he replied, "but actually, why not? I thought it would be fine."

Cassady was notorious for sharing his women with "bloodbrothers": He'd shared LuAnne with Kerouac, and at least one Denver girl with Hal Chase. Carolyn's mistake was to think she was special. When Jack and Neal began to resume their old, exclusive ways, she suffered "a vision of the future as an incessant repetition of the past." She made up her mind, however, not to go meekly into that future. Once again, Cassady was forcing a loved one to shed custom and conviction and to swim in a potentially destructive element.

The next evening, while Neal was working the railroad, Carolyn put the kids to bed and prepared Jack's favorite dinner of pizza and salad. There was wine and

candlelight and soft music, and she guilefully deterred
Jack from ascending to the attic. They sat on the daybed.
Jack hummed "My Funny Valentine," and Carolyn re-
called the first time they danced together in Denver. Jack
remembered that he wanted then to steal her away from
Neal. No further words or maneuverings were needed.

Carolyn and Jack were discreet, but Neal was
instantly aware that the friendship had altered. He was
neither angry nor indifferent, but all the more attentive
to Carolyn. It was as if he had facilitated the encounter
with his "brother" to make his woman interesting once
more, to renovate her charms. Whatever the case, the
result was a new season for Carolyn, suddenly the focus
of both men's attentions. She saw her housework and her
maternal tasks in a better light, now that she was
appreciated. Indeed, Jack and Neal took turns reading
Spengler and Proust aloud to her as she mopped or
tended to the children. She was even admitted to the
taped conversations that would be included raw in
*Visions of Cody*, the book that Kerouac was feverishly
writing in the Cassady attic. "I served whichever was in
residence, according to their individual requirements,"
Carolyn demurely recalled in *Heart Beat*.

Soon Ginsberg was writing *to her* (!) saying that
he knew he'd always been "a beat cocksucker" in her
imagination, but that he'd never meant her personal
harm. Carolyn was thrilled at being inducted into what
Allen called "the hazy circle, which itself knoweth itself
not." Newly confident, she tried exotic currents on her
own. She took a job as a camera girl at a strip of night

clubs in North Beach, San Francisco's Barbary Coast. But
she quickly realized, what with the hoods and homosexuals, that she was out of her depth. She found too that
she was not so keen about making the rounds with her
men. She didn't care for marijuana, everybody laughing
inordinately at dumb things, and she was dismayed by
Neal's blatantly making passes at other women in her
presence. Her excursions into Neal's "other world" helped
Carolyn define her own limits, and actually confirmed
her in her aspiration to a conventional marriage. She
persisted in thinking that Neal would come around in
time.

All in all, the five months Kerouac spent at 29
Russell Street were the most harmonious of the Cassadys'
long-troubled union. When Jack left in May 1952, to
complete his customary Mémêre-to-Neal-to-Burroughs-to-
Mémêre trajectory, the Cassady marriage returned to its
fallen condition. Neal lapsed once more into blankness,
and Carolyn into her role as the beleaguered heroine of
early English fiction.

The year 1953 proved to be momentous for the Beats.
Burroughs spent most of the year in the Amazon jungle
in search of the vaunted yage vine. After run-ins with
police in Panama and Bogotá, he finally made contact
with Indian holy men who prepared and consecrated the
drug, which caused him to envision larval beings squawk-
ing obscenely in a blue haze and surreal cities where
"the unknown past and the emergent future" met in "a
vibrating soundless hum." In exchanging junk for

hallucinatory drugs, Burroughs was beginning a turn-about. For eight years, he would say, he had been content merely to stare groggily at his big toe. Soon he would be writing Ginsberg, "The most dangerous thing to do is to stand still."

Burroughs had suffered a tragedy and a sea change. At a late-night party in Mexico on September 7, 1951, he had been tempted by his wife to stage a William Tell demonstration. Joan Burroughs balanced a champagne glass on her head and Bill, who most always while in Mexico carried a target pistol, fired from close range, putting a bullet through her brow. As a consequence of the killing, Burroughs lost custody of his children. As John Tytell has remarked in *Naked Angels*, he was effectively "freed from his past" and launched into a writing career that started with *Junkie* and that would hit a high point with *Naked Lunch*.

It was about this time that Kerouac observed in a letter that America is everywhere becoming "Bahaian." Indeed, Burroughs was not the only one who was "orienting" himself. Ginsberg wrote Cassady in May 1953, saying that he was spending all his free hours in New York libraries leafing through Chinese art books. He was beginning, too, to sample Zen Buddhism by reading D. T. Suzuki. Soon he would himself begin a trek to the Yucatan, the Occident's Orient.

Kerouac, meanwhile, was rebounding from a love affair with a part Negro, part American Indian woman whom he called "Mardou Fox." He treated the relationship—marked by competition with the new Beat *enfant,*

Gregory Corso—in *The Subterraneans*, which was committed to a teletype roll in just three autumn nights.
Seeking balm for his love and career disappointments,
Jack turned to Thoreau's *Walden*, which held him largely
with its Eastern allusions. He quickly obtained a copy of
Ashvagosha's *The Life of the Buddha* and found there
something of what he needed: He was especially struck
by the notion of "Repose Beyond Fate," a state he was
eager to achieve.

Equipped with just a smattering of Buddhism,
Kerouac arrived February 1954 at the Cassadys' new home
in San Jose, only to find that Neal had himself turned
East, more or less. He was spouting reincarnation and
karma and talking about atman entities and about the
etheric akasha essence, upon which is impressed a record
of every sound, movement, and thought since the beginning of the universe. He had come to embrace the
doctrine assocated with Edgar Cayce, the onetime Ken-
tucky farm boy turned clairvoyant, psychic healer, and
religious teacher. Cassady had found a copy of Gina
Cerminara's book on Cayce, *Many Mansions*, while parking an automobile some months earlier in 1953. (Neal
had incurred a serious injury to his foot at his railroad
job and was relegated, while awaiting the financial
settlement, to working parking lots.) He and Carolyn had
been transfixed, as had Kerouac with Buddhism, by
Cayce's explaining power and relevance to their lives.

Kerouac would later admit to Ginsberg that he
and Cassady were probably, ultimately, beholden to the
same "pusher." Yet there was a basic difference in the

two belief systems, which rang clear in the arguments, recorded by Carolyn, between Neal and Jack at the kitchen table in San Jose.

"But a *soul*, man, you are a soul; the soul is *you*, individual, special," Cassady argued. "The You you've been building from dozens of lives ... makin' it and blowin' it, see?"

"Pah! All life is suffering and pain," responded Kerouac, "the cause is *desire*. The world is all illusion.... nothin' means nothin' ... period!"

Jack objected to the *arriviste* aspect of Neal's prophet and compared him to "Billy Graham in a suit." More importantly, Kerouac, who increasingly longed for (but feared) annihilation, objected to "the residue of ego" in Cassady's newfound creed. Neal and Carolyn, for their part, disapproved of what they took to be Jack's nihilism. The two friends harangued one another for a couple of months, then finally invested their difference in a quarrel over who was to pay for pork chops, with the result that Kerouac moved to a greasy hotel in San Francisco.

Strictly speaking, Edgar Cayce was not a teacher but a "channel," an *idiot savant* who spoke oracularly from a deep sleep. His prophecy, a blend of Eastern detachment and Christian purposefulness, turned on twin tenets of reincarnation and karmic law. In Cayce's scheme, an individual soul evolves through successive lifetimes on earth toward the human perfection person- ified by Jesus. Reincarnation is, however, anything but easy unfoldment. Man, as in most religious systems, is fallen. Yet with Cayce, his corrupt condition does not derive from Adam and Eve's misdeed, but from the conduct of his anterior selves.

Reincarnation is informed by Karmic law: That is, sin and suffering are in cause-and-effect relationship. Reincarnation is a "wheel of justice," and justice is meted out in apposite, even witty ways. Thus if one is culpable in one life of selfishly thwarting others, in the next life he might suffer paralysis of the limbs. Or if he were guilty of sexual excess in an early life, he might subsequently be visited with epilepsy, a kind of burlesque of orgasm. Yet karmic justice is "continuitive" as well as retributive. If in one life a man fights a tendency to sadism, in the next he may well be spared this blot and its attendant guilt. The Cayce faithful are encouraged to be of service to others and to develop "Christ-consciousness," to recognize divinity in themselves, in order to attain merger with the Creative Energy of the Universe.

Cayce's impact on the Cassadys was powerful. They bought dozens of books that treated or spun out of the phenomenon. They went to lectures given by experts and joined study groups. For several years they attended guidance sessions with the deceased medium's son, Hugh Lynn Cayce. Divorce became all but unthinkable because Carolyn and Neal believed that the way to perfection would be shown them through their life together. Neal attempted once more to analyze his blankness and control his antisocial drives. He led his children in Christian prayers. He sought to convert hapless Jehovah's Witnesses when they came peddling their Watch Towers; he even proselytized in North Beach. The family named its cocker spaniel "Cayce."

It is not difficult to imagine why Neal found the Cayce doctrine so congenial. It did not stigmatize sex, as did Neal's "formative" religion, Roman Catholicism, but celebrated it in moderation. By suspending man in the perpetual present, the teachings effectively invented a here and now more enormous than even Neal could have dreamed. The assertion that the entity in this life continues and only partly corrects sins from past lives must have soothed Neal's guilt over *his* inability to be "responsible," over *his* many infidelities. Neal surely took heart to discover that life is "a vale of soul-making," and that the proper attitude, as he always knew, was to be "resigned but searching." Finally, given his taste for the awesome, he must have reveled in Cayce's "past-life readings," which have the quality of Cecil B. De Mille spectacular.

The readings Neal was given were eerily on the mark. In one set of spiritual recitals—which Carolyn likened to a "long prayer"—Neal's saintly qualities were embodied in lives spent among the Egyptians and Druids and with the soul who would become Abraham Lincoln. But it was an earlier set of physical-emotional readings that most affected Neal. Listening to it, he surely saw his current existence in lurid pageant flashing horribly before him.

In the six lives given, which were considered

pertinent to his present condition, he was: A Bedouin tribesman who was put to death for acts of treachery and deceit. An officer in Nebuchadnezzar's army who was publicly castrated for the crime of rape. An oriental peasant who loved his pathetic father, killed his brother, was plagued by bad dreams, became addicted to opium, and perhaps contracted syphilis. A hapless admirer of Jesus who was killed while attempting to pay tribute to the Son of God with a stolen gem. A Basque, married to Carolyn, who became a religious fanatic and a murderer. An Assyrian charioteer who effectively killed his own son and superior competitor, John Allen, when during a race the latter saw his father losing his balance and pushed him clear of the curved knives Neal had attached to his chariot to give himself lethal advantage over the opposition, when John consequently lost his own balance and fell into the knives.

These readings formed a mosaic portrait that was at once inspiring and chillingly faithful to Neal's worst fears about himself in his present life. There *was* hope: He was no longer vengeful or sadistic, not to mention murderous. Clearly, he was evolving with purpose, and yet his current unsavory aspect was reflected darkly, unsettlingly, in the mirror of the past lives. It was all there: his con-man tactics; his insatiable lust for speed, drugs, sex, risk; his sense of inferiority and masochism; his nightmares and hallucinations; his spiritual fanaticism, the futility of his best intentions, the imbalance of his body chemistry. It was all there, along with grisly turns on relationships with his father, brother Jimmy, Carolyn, and especially John Allen. It is no wonder that the readings left him awash in tears.

Neal would find some consolation in Cayce's admonition, "You have not failed yet." But his central problem was the business of "Christ-consciousness." "He couldn't think of himself as good, as an expression of God," said Carolyn. Neither, it appeared, could he believe in a New Testament deity. "As ye sow, so shall ye reap" and "God is not mocked" were his favorite quotes from the Bible. He sought converts for Cayce, talking up the divine in man, as if to convince himself.

Cassady was much taken in the middle and late fifties by the example of Starr Daily, who was a sort of flip side of Caryl Chessman. The pseudonymous Daily was billed on the evangelical circuit as "The Greatest Reformed Criminal in America." As a youth in the 1920s he had been a habitual criminal, seething with hate for society and for himself. While in prison, during a stay in solitary, Daily had a mystical experience and was born again, a lover of Christ and mankind. Cassady pored over Daily's books—*Release, Love Can Open Prison Doors,* etc.—and attempted to follow the ex-con's Pauline disciplines. Once he even managed an interview with Daily. All to no avail.

Grasping at straws in his cyclical effort to conform, to become "responsible," Cassady failed to see that Daily's case was essentially different from his own. For Neal, while he could not love himself, was already Christlike in his love of others. He was likened by one elderly friend, an astrologer, to a mythic figure called the Love Apple, a handsome man who gave himself to everyone in order to relieve human loneliness. "Neal is Christ walking in the doubts of the Garden of Whores," Ginsberg once wrote Kerouac. Indeed, all those persons who bore with Cassady with Joblike devotion, who resisted imposing upon him a grid of conventional expectation, all agreed that Neal was a paragon, a saint.

Furthermore, should Jesus have appeared to Cassady in a moment of vividness, it is not likely that the experience would have led to conversion. Unlike Starr Daily, Neal was an old hand at the "mystic spin" and would doubtless have greeted Jesus as he did other noumena: with "Yes, yes, yes."

Increasingly, Cassady would forgo the homiletic in favor of the occult side of Cayce. While Cayce led Carolyn to "positive thinking," to such practical religious groups as Unity, he led Neal to Gurdjieff and P. D. Ouspensky. "But at least Neal didn't talk about ectoplasm or materializations or astral planes with the children," said Carolyn. Indeed, more and more he led a double life. He continued to be the loving father and the adequate provider, but he settled deeper into drugs and spent more time at the races, more time with other—usually highstrung—women, more time in another faster and hospitable world.

In August 1954 Carolyn would catch Neal and Allen having sex together and would ask Allen to leave their house. As she drove Ginsberg to Berkeley, she would beg his understanding and forgiveness. A month later she would write him suggesting a return visit. Carolyn was still seeking counsel on how to live with Neal and was just beginning to come around to her most effective, if most anguishing, attitude. "All you have to do is keep your mouth shut," Hugh Lynn Cayce advised her. She had been praying for years that Neal would change, that he would mature. Now she was gradually learning to regard Neal with a semblance of his own professed "objectivity of emotionality," with what Cayce called "loving indifference."

Carolyn put up little fuss, when, late in 1955, Neal decided to move out of their home in Los Gatos and into San Francisco to live with girl friend Natalie Jackson. And she took him back in November in spite of Neal and Natalie's scam—in spite of their having forged her signature on stocks worth ten thousand dollars (the remaining portion of moneys the railroad paid Cassady in compensation for his foot injury), and of their blowing the cash at the race track while proving Neal's "system." Carolyn took Neal back when thirty-five-year-old Natalie—a fragile soul who was apparently unhinged by the race track episode—dressed in a bathrobe and climbed to the roof of her building, where she slashed her throat with glass from a broken skylight and fell three flights to her death.

Just weeks before Natalie took her life, the Beat vanguard mounted its first and most famous audition. At the Six Gallery, an old garage in San Francisco, five poets, introduced by Kenneth Rexroth, gave what have come to be regarded as historic readings. First Philip Lamantia recited the poetry of a late friend. Next Michael McClure read his poem "For the Death of 100 Whales." Gary Snyder and Philip Whalen would follow, but the third poet in the sequence was the one whose debut marked the evening. For the first time in public, Allen Ginsberg read "Howl," his shock assault on Moloch-ridden, madness-making, tight-assed America. It was, Lamantia recollected, "like bringing the ends of an electric wire together." Along with *On the Road*, "Howl" would galvanize a generation.

Neal attended the Six reading in his brakeman's uniform. Allen remembered him there in his watch and vest beaming with pride at "Howl," in which he appeared, of course, as "N.C., the secret hero of these poems, cocksman and Adonis of Denver." Unlike Kerouac, an ardent partisan who yelled "Go" at each successive poet, Cassady felt somewhat peripheral to the event. Peter Orlovsky, Ginsberg's new lover, later said that Neal approached him at the Six, saying, "Come over here, Peter, come stand next to me." When Orlovsky asked why, Neal said, "Well, I don't know anybody here." Although he was its muse, Cassady was not an integral part of the Beat movement when it made its percussive claim on the national attention.

By the time *On the Road* came out in 1957, Neal was still more peripheral to the Beat epicenter. He had finally been replaced in Ginsberg's affections by Orlovsky, and his relationship with Kerouac was largely over. In any case, all three men were greatly changed. Ginsberg

had found his own "naked" style and scandalous message; he had come to swim in the "uncharted rhetorical
invented seas" where Kerouac and Cassady had been
skinny-dipping for years. Ginsberg's life had begun to jell.
He was becoming that necessary figure, the public poet.
Kerouac, on the other hand, had been at once driven and
debilitated by his failure to get published after *The Town
and the City*. He had produced his most ambitious work
in the interim between the writing of *On the Road* and
its publication, but he had done so at a certain cost. He
was less and less the joyous protean sensibility who'd
extended himself to match strides with his "brother,"
Neal Cassady. Jack had always had a conservative, even a
redneck, side (indeed, a few years earlier, during the
Hollywood purge, he'd observed to Lucien Carr that
Senator Joseph McCarthy had "all the dope on the Jews
and the fairies"). Now he was becoming increasingly
reactionary, regressing to the narrow model of Leo, his
father. In the next several years, fame would undo him.
For nearly a decade he had hungered for recognition, but
when the public at last chose to take notice it would
choose to measure the least part of him. In forums and
on talk shows, he would be queried about drugs, kicks,
promiscuity. No one would understand or care to credit
the spiritual underpinnings of *On the Road;* interviewers
would regard him quizzically when he suggested that his
life and work constituted a single effort to force God to
pull back the veil and show Himself in the altogether. To
make matters worse, Jack purposely behaved on public

occasions like a Zen lunatic, countering the distasteful questions with koans and horseplay. Finally, to protect himself from the bitch-goddess, Success, he would don a "liquid suit of armor"—he would find a sapping strength in Muscatel and Tokay wine.

Neal was himself in the late fifties only in part the outsize hero of *On the Road*. He was more than ever self divided. Home with Carolyn, still trying intermittently to be the good bourgeois, he was uneasy about the glorification of his antic persona in Kerouac's book. He recoiled from the Beat stereotype which, Ginsberg later noted, "spread from head to head like trench mouth." "Excitement and movement mean everything [to the Beats]," said *Time* magazine. "Steady jobs and homes in the suburbs are for 'squares.'" Yet Neal was, with at least part of his person, working at being just that—a *square*. He took the furor over *On the Road* personally. Somewhat illogically, it upset him, according to Carolyn, that neither the fans nor the vilifiers of Dean Moriarty considered *his*, Neal Cassady's, work record—the ten years he'd put in as one of the Southern Pacific's best brakemen. It bothered him that he/Dean Moriarty was alternately dismissed and celebrated as a delinquent and a bohemian.

Meanwhile, away from home he was becoming something of a cult figure. In North Beach bars and coffeehouses he styled himself as Johnny Potseed, as marijuana central for the city of San Francisco. Yet his performance away from Los Gatos was similarly burdened. He was still weighed down with guilt over Natalie

Jackson's death and loathed himself more than ever. His
every act seemed to beg a judicious turn of the karmic
wheel. Retribution was not a long time coming.

On April 8, 1958, Cassady was arrested in San
Francisco for allegedly smuggling large quantities of Mexican marijuana on the railroad. Testimony was confined,
however, to a couple of joints he admitted offering two
men—undercover agents, it turned out—in trade for a
ride to work. Neal was kept in the city jail for a week,
until the grand jury decided the evidence was shaky and
released him. The very next day he was rearrested and
bail was set at twelve thousand dollars. He had taken the
first arrest calmly, but this time he was so wild that
Carolyn decided not to second-mortgage the house to
make his bond. She worried that Neal would jump bail
and forfeit the only thing she and the children had.

The local climate was hardly conducive to Neal's
getting a fair trial. The hometown paper, the San Jose
*Mercury*, quoted a San Francisco police inspector to the
effect that Cassady was a cog in "a pretty cozy operation"
doing thousands of dollars of illicit business. He was
identified, with unwitting acuity, as "the family type who
led a double life." For good measure, the reporter added
that Neal was a friend of "the controversial Allen
Ginsberg," whose poem "Howl" was "almost banned."
During the sentencing, Neal would not name his alleged
accomplices and was merely polite rather than penitent,
which induced the judge to bellow, "I don't *care* if there
is no evidence. I don't like his attitude!"

Cassady was given two terms of five years to life,
to run concurrently, which actually meant two years in

the penitentiary, not including the three months he'd already spent in the city jail. "God is not mocked," said Cayce. But He is Himself, apparently, not without a sardonic wit: Neal officially began his sentence on July 4, 1958, Independence Day.

His first stop was the medical facility at Vacaville. He somewhat controlled his furor over Carolyn's "treason," her failure to put up the house for his bail, and looked forward to their "Easter of new beginnings" in 1960. Meanwhile, he immersed himself in religious literature, the Bible, Thomas Merton, and books endorsed by Cayce, notably one called *Dweller on Two Planets*. "As for my soul," he wrote Carolyn, "you well know we both consider imprisonment an unparalleled opportunity to attain greater grace & I'm sensing this purging in ever greater amounts as I persevere in prayer & meditation." The example of Starr Daily glistening before him, he hoped to emulate the "splendid rebirth" of Saint Paul.

The three months he was in Vacaville, however, he anguished over his relatively manorial existence. He was doing what cons call fine time. He was suntanned and pampered, "what with daily showers, plenty of rest, good reading, weekly movies, gym, tops in food, & free rolling tobacco too!" He pictured the kids and Carolyn living in shame, poverty, and fear—and was not far from wrong.

Initially the children—aged ten, nine, and seven— and their mother were showered with attentions by the townspeople. Friends and mere acquaintances volunteered to cut the lawn, to baby-sit, to make the mortgage payment. Local stores cancelled bills, and groceries flooded in from every quarter. Cathy was treated to summer camp and Jami to swimming lessons. "It looks as tho all of this has been planned and timed," Carolyn wrote Ginsberg, cresting on her neighbors' benefactions and Neal's new dedication to reform. "We are actually happier than we've been in years tho of course ... I miss him terribly." For the first time in their life together, Carolyn would say, she knew just where Neal was and what he was doing.

What seemed at first to be Frank Capra comedy took a turn toward Dickensian pathos when the novelty of the Cassady plight wore off for the townsfolk. Carolyn began two years of struggle with the local welfare board (which, for one thing, suggested that she divorce Neal to get more benefits) and bouts of humiliation with assorted charities that singled the family out as "underprivileged." Adding to the burden was Carolyn's determination that the children not learn of Neal's imprisonment until they were older and he was out. Miraculously, they did not learn of his incarceration until high school.

After three months at Vacaville, Neal hoped to go to Soledad where, he said in a last bit of levity, "the kissing facilities are better." But the guards dressed him in snow-white pajamas, struck him in leg irons, and bused him to San Quentin, where he would be a fresh fish among 5,000-odd felons. He was planted in a 4½- by 7½- by 9½-foot cell. "To get some idea of what lying so encaged is like," he wrote Carolyn, "you might put car mattress in the bathtub, whereby making it softer, and if not as long, at least much cleaner than is my bug-ridden bunk; then bring in your 200 lb. friend, Edna, or the more negatively aggressive, Pam. Lock the door, & after dragging 11 rowdy kids into our bedroom to parallel the 1,100 noisy ones housed in this particular cell block; of course, in the bathroom, you must remove the toilet seat, towel racks, cabinet ... anything other than a small mirror & 4½" shelf ... remain almost motionless so as not to inadvertently irritate armed-robber-Edna, ponder past mistakes, present agonies & future defeats in the light of whatever insights your thus-disturbed condition allows."

The devotional habits Neal developed at Vacaville took on an obsessional quality in San Quentin. He began composing prayers to be said throughout the day, in addition to standardized morning and evening observances. He was especially proud of a litany in which he recited from memory the name of each of the 262 popes, from Peter to Pius XII. He also elaborately imagined his ordeal in prison as that of a postulant in a Cisterian monastery. He had read that the Cisterian candidate spent an initial ninety days somewhat as his three months in the San Francisco jail; then two years as a novice, which accorded with his term in the pen; and finally, three years under "simple vows," the equivalent of his parole period.

Numbers and numerology, *pattern* itself, had long been rife with metaphysical significance for Cassady. In prison, number, prayer, and incantation blended into one: a talisman to charm away evil, largely the loss of sanity. To withstand the hellish racket made by the "4-million-dollars worth of 1745 R.P.M. 68 × 72 inch hi-speed looms" in the prison textile mill—where it was his job to sweep the constantly collecting flug—Neal would shout into the roar every formula of devotion that he knew. Indeed, he discovered to his fascination that if he hurried through each known prayer he would find himself ready, exactly sixty minutes later, to begin a new cycle.

In San Quentin his life became allegory. His every act was freighted with karmic significance. When he pitched horseshoes in the yard his thought automatically turned to his weakness for the horses and gambling and instantly racked him with guilt over Natalie Jackson. When Jami innocently scribbled him a note saying "hay, hay" instead of "hey, hey"—*hay* being a cant term for marijuana—he felt the twist of "the sharp memory-knife" of the "vile weed" that put him in the pen. "Man everywhere meets himself," said Cayce.

This bleak trend of mind was countered, however, by another more positive inquiry into Meaning. It comforted him that he was, after all, named Neal: that is, Kneel. And though this would have brought him but small consolation, he entered a second remarkable period of letter writing. Indeed, for the first time his incorrigible taste for alliteration ("how this beat beatster beats a beat bastille") seemed warranted, even poignant. The tightly screwed, remorselessly self-echoing language squeezed onto the permitted five-by-seven inch ruled paper was only too appropriate to news from the abyss.

Worldly failure was always Cassady's most creative element, and, typically, he put his descent to use.

Gavin Arthur, grandson of the twenty-first president and comparative religion teacher at San Quentin, would later say that Neal was at his most sublime in prison. It was the one place where he could use his magnificent mind, said Arthur, adding that it was the only place Neal was not a slave to the "desire-body." The very first day of class, Arthur picked Neal out of a group of sixty inmates: Neal was shining with unearthly fire.

On July 4, 1960, the Cassadys celebrated Neal's independence. The belated "Easter of new beginnings" was, however, something of a farce. Neal had lost his good-paying, loosely structured railroad job and was forced into the physically draining and monotonous work of changing truck tires. He was denied the right to leave the county or to associate with old friends. Worse, he could not shake deep feelings of resentment. "He believed he was 'owed' the $10,000 worth of our investments he had lost at the track before his arrest," said Carolyn. He returned to the track repeatedly to "get even." His losses there and mounting traffic tickets only fueled his resentment and attendant guilt.

Naturally Cassady did not abide by the dictate of his parole, that he stay within the county. Once more he became a staple in North Beach. In addition, he started spending time in the Palo Alto area, stalking Stanford coeds. It was there that he fell in with Ken Kesey and a retinue soon to be known as the Merry Pranksters. To alter Kerouac's formulation, Neal was a phoenix risen to redeem a new generation.

# PART FOUR
# FASTESTMANALIVE

*"The Revolution Has Begun*—Stop giving your authority to Christ & the Void & the Imagination—*you are it,* now, *the God ...* you are *needed*—stop hiding yr. light in a bushel."

ALLEN GINSBERG in a letter to
Neal Cassady, December 4, 1960

Ken Kesey always felt bad that he, a legatee of the Beats, never sent Jack Kerouac the letters of praise he carried in his head. Had he and other sixties' debtors cut through polemic and fashion and properly made out Kerouac's distorted cry for help and answered it with gratitude and compassion, they might have prevented his decline.

Actually, Kesey might have made a difference, for he and Kerouac touched at a number of points. He also grew up in a largely blue-collar town—Springfield, Oregon—which was perhaps not dissimilar to Kerouac's Lowell. Like Jack, he was once a star athlete, a football player and a wrestler with a national reputation. Kesey's father was also a "man's man," though his stake in manliness was more salutary than Leo Kerouac's: He believed in rites of passage, in physical contests between father and son, and went so far as to stage them. Like Jack, Ken had a mother and brother with whom he was close, but neither presented the complications of Mémère or Gerard.

115

During high school Kesey pursued the sort of life that is so sweetly evoked in the movie *American Graffiti*, characterized by oxford-cloth shirts, V-8 engines, drive-ins, and rock 'n' roll. Raised a low-rent populist—he was the first in his family to complete high school, much less college—the young Kesey confined his reading to Zane Grey, Edgar Rice Burroughs, and comic books, especially Captain Marvel, his answer to Kerouac's The Shadow. Billy Batson, the orphan-newsboy, was taken by a mystic guide deep into unknown subway tunnels where he met an ancient Egyptian wizard dedicated to foiling evil. Shazam! and little Billy was turned into "the world's mightiest mortal," Captain Marvel, who was barrel-chested like Kesey himself, who was a somewhat goofy but serious superhero given to the epithet, "Holy moley!"

While Kerouac was always at odds with authority, Kesey was a model youth, in the Jaycee sense of the phrase. He was also revered by his peers and was voted most likely to succeed in his senior year—a prophecy he fulfilled at the University of Oregon, where he starred in college plays as well as on the wrestling mat and where, true to the *Our Town* pattern, he married high school sweetheart Faye Haxby in 1956. Actually, his one eccentric act during the undergraduate years was to take up writing, an unanticipated interest that brought him at age twenty-four, in 1959, to Stanford University and to a new and increasingly disaffected view of things. He was fascinated by the scene in nearby North Beach and by the Beat idea itself: the anomie and the kicks, the confusion of the sacred and the profane.

In Palo Alto, Ken and Faye landed on Perry Lane, a prototypal fifties bohemian enclave, where Kesey ran into a psychology student named Vik Lovell, who introduced him to Freudian thought and advised him of experiments with "psychomimetic" drugs going on at the Veterans Hospital in Menlo Park: twenty dollars a session for taking psilocybin, mescaline, IT-290, Ditran, LSD-25. In the spring of 1960 Kesey, a newly overhauled jock who'd never been drunk but that one night in his Oregon fraternity before his wedding, gave himself up to science and medical progress. Nothing would ever be the same again.

Within a few weeks he would buy his first ounce of grass. Within six months he was working as a psychiatric aide at the hospital, the midnight-to-eight shift, hooking down double-aught capsules of pure mescaline and feverishly mopping the floors when the night nurse came by so to camouflage his gondola-sized pupils. Withal, he was capitvated by the patients, by the arcane workings of their minds. Merely by taking the least bit of LSD, Kesey found that he could toss word salad with the most far-flung inmate. He discovered that by treating his mind with chemicals he could block out preconception; ergo, Truth could emerge, unmanacled and full blown. "In the antiseptic wilderness of the Menlo Park V.A. Hospital," he later wrote, "I cleared a space and rigged a runway for my muse to take the controls."

One day during the summer of 1960, while Kesey was primed with peyote, an unlikely "muse" taxied into view. Amid the faces from the hospital that repeatedly besieged him on his trips, that begged him to tell their story, there appeared a new face. It was the high-cheekboned, ruddy visage of an Indian, "Chief Broom"— this even though Kesey had never so much as met a Native American. He was compelled to rewrite his new novel about the acutes and the chronics of a mental ward, which he was typing during the early-morning shift, from the Chief's own (cactus-)clouded point of view. The result, *One Flew Over the Cuckoo's Nest*, was a moral tale about a logger-roustabout named Randle Patrick McMurphy who delivered the inmates of a psychiatric ward from the grasp of a control-crazed overseer, Big Nurse. It was a cartoon-lucid psychodrama featuring an outsize antihero who sacrificed his life to save his "mad" disciples, who delivered his faithful not by restoring them to what generally passes for sanity, but by bringing them to see the vicious chauvinism of society. In the moving climax, McMurphy liberated the Chief himself, who—in this allegory of consciousness—stood for the repressed "alien vision" in all normal, socially processed Americans.

Broad of chest, red hair boiling out from under his cap, McMurphy was clearly a projection of Kesey's boyhood fantasy of his own superheroism. And yet ... McMurphy's extra-physical lineaments are uncannily familiar. The first thing Chief Broom notices about him is his laugh, which laps at the bounds of the ward: "I realize all of a sudden it's the first laugh I've heard in years." Next the Chief observes McMurphy's hands, which

are large and beat up, and his proletarian smell of sweat
and work. Always candid, in his way, McMurphy intro-
duces himself to the awestruck inmates as "a gambling
fool" and promptly flashes a deck of pornographic playing cards. His initials are R.P.M.—speed itself—and
instantly he is doing myriad things at once. "The way he
talks, his wink, his loud talk, his swagger," says Chief
Broom, "all remind me of a car salesman or stock
auctioneer—or one of those pitchmen you see on a
sideshow...." McMurphy is a con man, plain and disturbingly unsimple. His speech is often a hurtling spiel. He
has no regard for his or other people's safety. He seems to
alter the very flow of time on the ward. To cap matters,
he has been labeled a psychopath by society's psychoana-
lytic vestry: It seems that he is, among other things,
"overzealous" in his sexual relations.

Having finished *Cuckoo's Nest* in the spring of
1961, Kesey journeyed to Oregon to help his brother start
a creamery. He returned to Palo Alto in the summer of
1962, just months after his novel had been published to
handsome praise almost everywhere. Pulling up to the
old cottage on Perry Lane, he and Faye descried an antic
figure on their lawn—a man with an athletic build,
maybe in his late thirties, dressed in a T-shirt and chinos
and bobbing up and down as if he were a boxer, batting
great blue flirtatious eyes and jabbering, jabbering. "Yes,
yes, yes, why hello Chief..."

The meeting was clearly ordained. Kesey had
dreamed Cassady first, had imagined him into being—
with the usual distortions of dreamwork, of course—as

Randle Patrick McMurphy. Neal had discovered the book and had felt summoned by its author. It was fitting that, virtually from the start, Cassady called Kesey "Chief," for his unarticulated mission with this new "brother" and the motley crew that was beginning to collect around him was to assist in their release into "alien vision," that hairy space where all the wild things are.

A few months after Neal met Kesey, Carolyn decided to file for divorce. Children in tow, she had gone one fall weekend to Pacific Grove to attend a Cayce retreat. Leaving Neal at home alone was, in her mind—ever that of the heroine of early English fiction—to be something of a test. She had left him at home and to his own device on just one other occasion since he'd been released from San Quentin.

On her return that Sunday, she entered the empty house to find what she would liken to "a macabre version of Goldilocks and the Three Bears." The living room was all right, but the bed in their room had been mysteriously stripped. She found the sheets, splotched with blood, stuffed loosely in the washer. Meanwhile she had a look at the patio, which was strewn with garbage and overturned chairs; at the pool, which was gorged with soggy toys; and at Johnny's room, which seemed to have been hit by rolling thunder—notably, a highly prized racing car system which was reduced to twisted bits of metal. She had heard that Neal's latest mistress had a two-year-old son.

When Neal showed up several days later, Carolyn
stated her intention. He did not argue, especially as she
intimated, somewhat falsely, that she would be marrying
another, older, and more secure man. Neal knew the
man and quietly conceded that the divorce and her
remarriage would doubtless benefit the kids.

When Carolyn wrote Kerouac to tell him of her
action, Jack responded with dismay. He also advised her
at length on how to deal with the growing emotional
problems of twelve-year-old Johnny, his namesake, who
was said to be a genius but was not performing well in
school. "Encourage him to write little novels in his
room," wrote Jack, "give him plently of solitude and time
to dream. DONT BUG HIM WITH AMERICAN P.T.A.
FIDDLEFADDLE BUSY BODY SCHEMES which are only
suitable for mediocrities who don't know what to do
with themselves! Let him dream!" Jack was, of course,
commenting with little subtlety on Carolyn's marriage-
long campaign to domesticate Neal. Yet Carolyn had
recognized for some time that she was, where Neal was
concerned, always in good part an instrument of the PTA
mentality. "I'd now done what society expected," she said
after filing suit in the summer of 1963. "I had condemned ... retaliated with divorce, and it brought me
little consolation."

His job with the railroad gone, and now his
marriage, Neal had lost his stake in the world of getting
and spending, in what Kesey called "the Combine" and
Ginsberg "the syndrome of shutdown." Soon he was a

fixture at Kesey's new, secluded, and bizarrely outfitted
log house in La Honda, fifteen miles from Palo Alto. Hi-fi
speakers riffing jazz were mounted on the roof, crazy
paintings were tacked on trees, and weird mobiles and
mirrors depended from branches in the surrounding
redwood forest. The woods had promises to share: They
were rigged to jar the psychedelically prepped mind into
satori. It was all part of what Kesey called The Neon
Renaissance, a rubric he attached to the efforts of the
cultural vanguard to locate a new reality now that the
old one was "riddled with radioactive poison." Ornette
Coleman in music, Ann Halprin in dance, the New Wave
in movies, Lenny Bruce in comedy, Wally Hendrix in art,
William Burroughs in writing—they were all comrades
unaware and at the ramparts. And Kesey's portion in
"the revolution" was to attract and hone cohesive a
company of psychedelic guerrillas—a group, *Whole Earth
Catalog*er Stewart Brand would say, that had the bravado
of an elite military unit. It was in them all to be
superheroes, to take risks, and to have great fun in the
process. It was in them, in a phrase, to be holy goofs.

  In the spring of 1964 Kesey and a dozen renaissance men and women climbed aboard a 1939
International Harvester bus mandalaed with Day-Glo and
equipped with a PA system, and they began a trip that
was an inspired mock-up of the transcontinental jaunts
of Sal Paradise and Dean Moriarty. In most every respect
the latent content of Kerouac and Cassady's comparatively
modest picaresque fantasy was made manifest, turned
inside out, and projected onto a larger screen. Where the

Beats (mostly inadvertently) baited the squares while
seeking furtive pleasures, the Merry Pranksters rode
through America "tootling" the uninitiated: They climbed
to the top of the bus, waved make-believe batons, and
"played" the gaping public as though it were music of
their composition, or they drove the bus backward
through cities consecrated to Barry Goldwater, filming
the whole business and thereby (con)scripting the astonished squares to "their movie." Where Kerouac and
Cassady hung out in jazz clubs and Kerouac fervently
wished he were a Negro, "feeling the best the white
world had offered was not enough ecstasy," the Pranksters drove onto a segregated beach outside New Orleans
and conjured the initially hostile black bathers to form a
circle around the bus and to gyrate to the Pranksters'
own funky sounds. Where Kerouac and Cassady, hurt into
taking to the road by mad America, implicitly "healed"
themselves as they went along (in critic Leslie Fiedler's
phrase) "by play-therapy," the Pranksters overtly structured their events as encounter sessions and meta-games.
LSD had disclosed to them what psychologists such as
Thomas Szasz and Eric Berne had come to perceive from
a more sober vantage: that Americans were infected with
"games" that shriveled the soul—games to attain wealth,
status, and power. The antidote, the Pranksters felt, was
not in withdrawal, as Timothy Leary suggested, to the
frictionless realm of "non-game." Rather it was in cutting
through the rigmarole with straight and often perilous
talk: If you desired someone, you told him and risked a
put-down; if you disliked the number somebody was

running you said so and risked dissension. The antidote lay, as well, in rendering society's games innocuous by *goofing* on them—that is, by bullshitting the bullshit. Thus the Pranksters invented a pastime of their own called "Power," a combination of spin the bottle and king of the hill that gave the victor absolute authority for thirty minutes to require everyone to do his prankish bidding. It was a "meta-game" that brought forward and mock-seriously treated, and thereby defused, every human being's infant wish for total control.

At the wheel during the journey east—which was timed so the merry company could arrive in New York for the publication of Kesey's second book, *Sometimes a Great Notion*—was Cassady. He was the road-happy Cassady of old, raised from a decade's ashes and re-named Speed Limit. He performed in much the same fashion this time out as he did fifteen years earlier with Kerouac: A manic Baedeker, he ticked off the sights as they came and went from his windshield ("there's a barber going down the highway cutting his hair at 500 miles a hour, you understand"); coming up over the Blue Ridge Mountains he switched off the ignition and ca-reered all the way down without once applying his brake; when the tires gave or the motor sputtered he got out the lug wrench or dove under the hood. He was the rock upon which a new church was being founded, he was reliable and responsible in a way he could never be in Carolyn's world.

If during the voyage to New York, Neal scarcely seemed to need sleep, it was because he was perpetually "cranked." He was becoming more and more addicted to amphetamine. He had been acquainted with the drug since the late forties, when Kerouac and Burroughs were experimenting with Benzedrine, when Joan Burroughs was wadding the innards of inhalers and knocking back a considerable number each day. It is difficult to say exactly when Neal became a dedicated user—probably just after prison, when his anger and self-loathing were at a peak. Yet it is not hard to see why he chose amphetamine: The drug works on the central nervous system to ease depression and to give the user a sense of physical and verbal prowess. For Cassady, speed was an equalizer: It dispelled the past and widened the vibrations of the present.

In the sixties, in most cases, acid heads and speed freaks divided into conflicting camps. LSD was not addictive, whereas amphetamine was to the point where the hard-core user spent much of his time in the sleaziest forms of hustling, especially after 1963, when Methedrine ceased to be sold over the counter. The acid head, by and large, saw his experience in a religious light and tended to denigrate the grubby ego trip of the amphetamine user. Generally the A-head was brought down from his polychromed nirvana by the speed freak's wired kinetics and logorrhea.

The Pranksters, celebrants of LSD, were attracted to Cassady, speed freak, for a number of reasons. First and least, he was Dean Moriarty, living legend. Secondly and importantly, Neal was in his own person a reproach to a terminally games-ridden society which could find no use for his eccentric genius—a society which almost whittled him down to comfortable size during the fifties and which banished him to prison at the turn of the decade. "[Cassady's] was the yoga," Kesey would say, "of a man driven to the cliffedge by the grassfire of an entire nation's burning material madness." What engaged the Pranksters, above all, was just *how* Neal comported himself on that burning "cliffedge."

The first acid trips had been shell-shattering ordeals that destroyed the Pranksters' frame of normal reference, stripped them of conventional notions of time and space and good and evil, and left them feeling naked and vulnerable but ecstatically convinced of their godlike potential. The LSD experience is, in objective terms, comparable to traditional mystic experience. It is a chemical shortcut through the Looking Glass to a state of awareness more diligently achieved by masters of Zen or Yoga through ritualized fasting, concentration, breathing exercises, incantation, and dancing. Sometimes called "instant Zen," acid transports the experiencer to a place where he feels himself to be in transactional relation to the universe—where, in the authoritative words of Alan Watts, "you feel that you are something being done by the universe, yet that the universe is equally something being done by you."

Many of the Pranksters believed that they were being supernaturally tampered with on a daily basis. The landscape was littered with portents. Sometimes the bus would get up and run by itself. Objects that had been missing for weeks, from wrenches to roach clips, would spring into view at the precise moment they were most needed. The Pranksters suddenly discovered themselves to be endowed with unearthly abilities: They could all, for example, routinely find things in the dark. "We were blind," said Mountain Girl, "but we had eyes in our feet. It set our heads swimming." Increasingly, they were coming to believe that they were in I-Thou relation to the universe, and their immediate concern was to make the most of it.

Put simply, the Pranksters looked to Cassady for tacit instruction on *how to behave in a post-LSD world.* "Neal was so far ahead of time," said Wavy Gravy, onetime protégé of Lenny Bruce and mainstay of the Hog Farm commune, "that he'd point for those of us who were just struggling to be with the moment." "At his purest," said Jerry Garcia, leader of the famed Prankster band, The Grateful Dead, "Cassady was a tool of the cosmos." Indeed, the Pranksters found Neal to be so tightly synched that he had precognitive powers to rival his beloved Edgar Cayce. Some of it was show biz, most of it was not. Just one of his many psychic routines was to rattle off the serial number of a dollar bill whenever anyone for whatever reason pulled one out. Often he would get the whole number, all ten digits. Sometimes he would predict for a gathering the gender, physical type, and mission of the next person to enter the room— or, on the road at night, he might announce that the still unharbingered vehicle coming the other way was a truck with just one working headlight. Invariably he was right. Ann Murphy, Cassady's main consort during the Prankster years, joined others in saying that to travel with Neal was to voyage in and out of parallel universes. On one trip east, she and Neal saw the same waitress in each of several cafés along their route, and, upon their arrival in New York, saw the same women, wearing Lanz dresses, that they'd just left behind in Los Gatos. Kesey himself would say that there were no "accidents" where Cassady was concerned: On those rare occasions when sure-handed Neal dropped the four-pound sledgehammer he was forever tossing, it was because there were bad vibrations in the room and he was moved to break them up.

Cassady was so firmly "in the zone" that he was, by all reports—by reports *both* acid-biased and acid-free—capable of carrying on several conversations on different levels at the same time. On one level he would be talking about what happened to him that day, while on another he would answer questions thrown at him from various spots in the room. His way of handling these questions was not to pull up short, or even really to divert his conscious attention, but to secrete three-and four-word responses into his flow. In some cases Neal would address himself to questions that were not formed aloud but that he picked up telepathically. In addition he had the unsettling, if flattering, faculty of resuming conversations from days earlier at precisely the place where they were discontinued.

"The first time I met Neal in the early sixties I couldn't figure out why Kesey was so excited about him," said Gordon Lish, a self-described square who has never taken LSD, who has been an editor at *Esquire* and is one today at Alfred A. Knopf. "He seemed pleasant enough but nothing special. The next time my wife and I saw him was at a party. We were talking to him when all of a sudden he started to recapitulate the talk going on around us and to comment on it, even while he was keeping up his end of our conversation. It was breathtaking.

"I got to know him quite well after that, since he used to stay at my house in Burlingame. He had without doubt one of the greatest minds I've ever known—certainly the quickest intelligence. And I've known Nobel Prize winners—James Watson, for one."

In the sixties, sped by amphetamine, Neal's headlong conversation evolved into what came to be celebrated all along the coast as Cassady's "rap." What Ginsberg once knew as his "excited, high fraternal talk" transmuted into what Kesey called Neal's "careening, corner-squealing commentary on the cosmos." It was, in a sense, just an older Dean Moriarty "digging" out loud, patching together "gloats of knowledge" for a new generation, up a notch and with greater amplitude. "It was forties stuff," said Robert Stone, Kesey's friend from Stanford and the author of *Dog Soldiers*. "It was old-time jail and musician and street patter." It was American-Denver talk, what Kerouac liked to think of as Okie drawl, but with free-lancing Proustian detail.

Invariably, Cassady's rap incorporated the same themes: cars and race-car driving, music and musicians, Edgar Cayce and the world of parapsychology. And interspersed were strange bits and pieces, pop allusions, stuff about centrifugal force and thermodynamics, the odd truth glistening mesmerically in the greater molten conglomerate. Ever since grammar school in Denver, Neal had been collecting useless verities. "Related, or unrelated, if it was fact, I knew it," he once wrote Ginsberg. "Important or unimportant, whether the amount of coffee grown in Brazil last year, or the weight ot Trotsky's brain, I dealt with facts." Between the ages of seven and fourteen Neal would seize the school day by running to the front of the classroom to ask the teacher if this fact or that was not so. One rare teacher, who did not view Neal as merely disruptive, was so impressed that she had him promoted midyear to the next grade. Yet until clearing his channels with amphetamine, until locating his Prankster role as "hipologuist," Cassady had never been able to properly showcase his extravagant powers. He needed a vehicle to bring his prodigious soul into full activity and an audience addled in the same way he was.

He needed an audience that could follow and savor an unrehearsed 30-minute performance that sped flat-out from naughty anecdote:

> *Double-clutching Winnemucca, speed or endurance,*
> *six days it was, finally she grabbed the Vicks*
> *Vaporub instead of the Vaseline, that's what ended it*

To zany news flash:

> *Logical positivism on a great increase at UCLA,*
> *recently they got Alcindor but no water polo, so what*
> *are we going to do?*

To reflexive commentary on the performance itself:

> *Ten miles an hour, we're in a great four-wheel drift,*
> *loose, ya know, everybody in this audience has a right*
> *foot, but I can't heel and toe, I'm double left!*

To parodic blue movie:

> *"But, Nell?"*
> *"Now see here, hard dick! My wife is a medical*
> *secretary, she works for a stiff Doctor Peck ... "*

To final resolution in patented Cassady wisdom:

> *The embryo, you know, always goes through the fish*
> *stage, but we didn't until ape-late. Christ-Adam helps*
> *us out so the Cyclops don't win the unicorn brew.*
> *We're here to experience and punctuate evolution, the*
> *little toe, we'll beat it though.*

Cassady's rap was the Saint Vitus' dance of his soul patterned with rebop, delivered in a hoarse self-amused voice somewhere between the Kingfish and Popeye the sailor man, and shouldered into being by an artist of physical motion with the comic aplomb of Buster Keaton. It was a convoy of routines and ideas chasing one another down the pike until (to quote a favorite sound effect) *smash! 'n' blasta-smashuss,* the car wreck of the mind issuing not in "accident" or whimsy but in Cassady *sententia,* something very much like necessary wisdom: "Christ-Adam helps us out so the Cyclops don't win the unicorn brew. We're here to experience and punctuate evolution...." Or as he once counseled Kesey and Co. in another rap: "Whatever's in the way is gonna join you. They ain't fighting *against* you, *remember* that son, all they can do is make you look sheepish.... Always tell by the fear in the belly how limited y'arre."

Cassady the inspired rapster was no mere Ouija in the grip of the Oversoul. On the one hand, to be sure, he presupposed a certain immunity: As he told Kerouac, he was convinced that "everything will be taken care of for us" (or "Whatever's in the way is gonna join you"). Yet on the other hand, as Carolyn often observed, "He was asking for it all the time" (or "Always tell by the fear in the belly how limited y'arre"). He was constantly daring fate or the deity to rein him in. He was, alternately, Abraham and Ahab, and nowhere did his paradoxical attitude better show itself than when he was wheeling and braking Detroit iron.

"When you went riding with him," said Jerry Garcia, "it was to be as afraid as you could be, to be in fear for your life. You'd be driving along in some old Pontiac or Buick, one of those cars Neal was always borrowing—with no brakes. You'd be racing through San Francisco at fifty or sixty miles per hour, up and down those streets with blind corners everywhere and he'd cut around them in the wrong lane and make insane moves in the most intense traffic situations and you'd just be amazed that people weren't getting killed. He could see around corners. And while he was doing this he'd be talking to everybody in the car at once and dialing in the radio and fumbling with a roach."

"Neal felt when he was at the wheel of a car," said Mountain Girl, "that his eyes were registering events ahead of the car at a certain rate and he was perceiving them at a certain rate and it takes a certain number of microseconds for the impulses to travel from the eyes to the brain and get processed and get down to the hand to turn the wheel. He was very sensitive to those tiny fragments of time. He was intimate with time."

Inevitably flagged down by the police, Cassady would abruptly change ratios. Giving over, for the moment, his furious "transaction" with the supernatural establishment, he would be genial, docile to mundane authority. *Too genial, too docile,* one might think, if one knew better. Yet the average cop could not possibly know better. There was no reason for him to anticipate someone as canny and beforehand as Cassady, someone who could shift from Ahab to Abraham—or better still, from Prometheus to Step 'n' Fetchit—without noticeably clutching.

Neal's initial strategy would be to try one of the more standard excuses: "Yes sir, why of course you're right. But my wife, y'see, she's in the hospital." Failing that, the next option was his famous "wallet show." Under the pretext of reaching for his license he would root through a billfold gross with mementos and semi-official-looking documents. As if by accident, he would produce a series of photos of Cathy, Jami, and Johnny, and—rapping the whole time, naturally—would direct his commentary toward the joys of parenting or maybe the trials thereof and what kids were coming to in this permissive age. Or else he'd fetch his Southern Pacific brakeman pass and thereby find occasion to dilate on the virtue of sweat and honest labor and perhaps, in the process, insinuate a blue-collar bond with the unwitting fuzz. All the while he would be reading the cop for telltale signs of softening.

These tactics failing, or not possible under the circumstances, he might resort to bold-faced candor and trust in the raw mania of the moment. Once, caught doing a U-turn in downtown Santa Cruz, Neal was confronted with an upholder of the law who knew straight off that he was wired. On what? the cop wanted to know. "Obitrol, office, obitrol," Neal answered. When the cop demanded to see the drugs, Neal compliantly reached into both his pockets and pulled out dozens of pills, simultaneously spilling change everywhere. Engrossed exclusively by this new turn of events, Neal quickly shoved the pills back into his pants and began to run in widening circles scooping up the change. His orbit grew bigger and bigger until finally, witnesses said, he just kind of faded into the distance, leaving the law standing there helpless and agape and ignorant that the perpetrator's license had long since been revoked.

Late in the evening of April 23, 1965, federal agents under the leadership of noted San Francisco nark William Wong descended upon Kesey's place in La Honda. The raid was not much of a surprise. The feds had been watching the house from the woods since late 1964, shortly after the merry band returned from its magical mystery tour to the East Coast. The Pranksters had rather enjoyed the supposedly covert surveillance and, naturally, improved upon the situation by "tootling" the stake-out: They mounted a huge sign on the house which said, WE'RE CLEAN, WILLIE! In the end just two Pranksters, Kesey and Page Browning, were hit with charges that stuck for possession of marijuana (LSD was not yet illegal). But they stayed free on bail for months while their lawyers haggled with the courts at the county seat in Redwood City.

The drug bust provided Kesey with a forum in the press, where he was referred to as a "hipster Christ" or "modern mystic" after the fashion of Jack Kerouac and William Burroughs. He told the reporters that he had stopped writing and that he was devoting his energies to a sprawling avant-garde movie with the title, *Intrepid Traveler and His Merry Pranksters Leave in Search of a Cool Place*. "I am not writing a third book," he said to one reporter, "because writers are trapped by artificial rules. We are trapped by syntax.... Even *Cuckoo* seems an elaborate commercial." At the time he made this statement Kesey was widely regarded as one of the country's top young novelists. But in his mind his own best effort, *One Flew Over the Cuckoo's Nest*, had been daunted by *the real thing*. "I saw that Cassady did everything a novel does," he would say, "except that he did it better because he was living it and not writing about it."

LSD and Cassady were a ways-and-means committee of two. Together they convinced the Pranksters that anything could be accomplished with sheer "mental power": that is, if they would give up any lingering concerns about looking foolish or being safe, if they would dare to trip along Cassady's burning "cliffedge." "Faith doesn't come from security," Kesey said. "It comes from survival."

In subsequent months the Pranksters entered into a series of epochal events that are chronicled at length by Tom Wolfe in *The Electric Kool-Aid Acid Test*. On August 7 they delivered themselves into what seemed certain peril when, through the offices of Hunter S. Thompson, they arranged to entertain the dread hippie-stomping Hell's Angels. It was an occasion that seemed to be further imperiled by the presence of East Coast Jewish intellectuals—a stomach-turning combination of attributes to Angel tastes—Allen Ginsberg and Richard Alpert, and of the local police, who milled restively on the periphery. But acid and chutzpah and sheer "mental power" saved the day, and the skull-emblazoned lion lay down with the Day-Glo lamb.

On October 16 Kesey, who was rapidly becoming a figure of prominence in the counterculture, was scheduled to speak at one of the first large anti-Vietnam War rallies in Berkeley. The idea was that thousands of students would listen to dozens of firebrand speakers who would rouse them to such a pitch that they would carry their protest over to the Oakland Army Terminal. In the organizers' minds, Kesey was a name who would attract demonstrators, a natural for the job along with such earnest, traditional leftists as Paul Jacobs and

M. S. Aroni. What the brain trust had not counted on
was the Cassady legacy: *goofism*.

The Pranksters arrived late at the demonstration.
They were dressed in rainbow-colored combat helmets
and nutty military outfits. The bus, decorated with
swastikas, American eagles, red crosses, etc., was trans-
formed into a zany send-up of a war wagon. As it turned
out, Kesey was the penultimate speaker, and he stunned
the multitudes and outraged the organizers by saying in
his leisurely down-home voice: *"You know, you're not
gonna stop this war with this rally, by marching....
That's what they do.... They hold rallies and they
march.... They've been having wars for ten thousand
years and you're not gonna stop it this way.... You're
playing ... their game...."* In a final mystifying gesture of
effrontery, Kesey put a harmonica to his mouth and
honked out a few bars of "Home on the Range."

"Fighting the system is serious business," the old-
guard radical lawyer reminds the goofy hero of one of
Tom Robbins's novels. On the contrary, says the hero, a
prototypal period outlaw, "it's serious business that
*creates* the system." Robbins, Abbie Hoffman, Kesey, and
other frivolous sixties "revolutionaries" were heirs, direct
and indirect, of Neal Cassady, whose example they drank
in in the white light of LSD. The point, said Kesey—who
apparently sapped the momentum that day from the
Berkeley antiwar march—was not to "go for the fried ice
cream," that is, not to play society's game. The Cassady
way was to exorcise the whole glum business by running

silly circles around it, by at once fading into a more congenial space and "cartooning" the war and its mentality out of existence.

Kesey and friends were in 1965 a fairly solitary company, at odds not just with their political brethren on the Left but with their fellow apostles of LSD, notably with the "high priest" himself, Timothy Leary. Both Leary and Kesey were keen to free themselves of their social conditioning, to follow the dictates of their internal blueprints. But whereas Leary retired to a serene Victorian mansion in Millbrook, New York, founded the League for Spiritual Discovery, worried about "set" and "setting" (i.e., internal and external decor) for the LSD trip, and sought to achieve an Olympian perspective on the marionette show of life, Kesey lived in a neonized log house in La Honda, was Chief to a bunch of paisleyed nut cases, and worked at creating electric, soul-boggling events in the interest of standing naked at the cosmic synapse. "Dropping out is the hardest yoga of all," said Leary. "Make your drop-out invisible." Don't drop *out*, said Kesey. Drop *in* on our alter-reality. And tell the world about it, he added, even as the Pranksters posted handbills throughout the Bay area asking, "CAN *YOU* PASS THE ACID TEST?" and advertising Neal Cassady and others as celebrity participants in multimedia fetes that with any luck would change your life.

More than a dozen Acid Tests were held during 1965 and 1966 in private homes, warehouses, and ballrooms in Santa Cruz, San Jose, Muir Beach, Palo Alto, San Francisco, Los Angeles, Portland, even Mexico. They were

wonderlands of gadgetry, what with all the tape machines, the movie and video projectors, light machines,
microphones, and speakers. The participants were encouraged to come not as they were but as they would be:
Kesey, for example, donned the tights of a superhero,
while Paul Foster went wrapped entirely in gauze with
just two eyeholes which he covered with sunglasses and
with a sign around his neck saying, "You're in the Pepsi
Generation and I'm a pimply freak." The Tests were mass
turn-ons. Thousands of people in a single evening would
drop acid or quaff glasses of Kool-Aid shot with 150
milligrams of "white lightning" and then would wait for
the floor to change colors.

Typically, at a Test there would be four pillars of
energy: The Grateful Dead whorling their "acid rock";
Kesey and his lieutenant, Ken Babbs, extemporizing (à la
Cassady) into the microphones; Wavy Gravy, the minister-
ing angel, guiding the terrified and the catatonic through
bum trips; and Cassady himself. Now and then Neal
would take a turn fugueing at the microphones, but
mostly he was mike-shy and chose to work the perimeter.
While a portion of the acid initiates would be glued to
the hipalogue at center stage, and another portion would
be transfixed by the Prankster movie that flickered on the
walls or by the freeze frames of the strobe light or by the
noodling sounds of The Dead, a few strays would invariably join Neal in, say, scrutinizing garbage. "Cassady
would pick stuff off the floor, cigarette packs, or whatever," said Wavy, "and he would read it like Native
Americans read meaning in natural things: the way

mushrooms or mosses grow, the ways rocks are arranged. It was the world as *I-Ching*."

"Neal was often more interesting than the main
event of the moment," said Jerry Garcia. "He was like the
guy who was out picking pockets while the man on the
platform was selling snake oil."

According to the Pranksters, Cassady was at the
top of his form during the Acid Tests. The Tests meant
constant travel, constant interchange with new talent, a
constant round of talk and activity. But nothing more
was demanded of Neal than that he be himself: He was
an attraction, not a promoter or a planner. On those
occasions when the pressure to perform got too heavy, he
kept his composure by pranking his adulators' expecta-
tions. He might, for example, trap the neophyte A-head
anxious to learn to read the world as *I-Ching* by blatantly
poking through the evening's rubble with a flashlight. He
would wait for the eager novice to ask *him*, the Keeper of
the Flame, "Hey, Neal, what are you looking for?" so he
might respond, "Somebody to talk to."

Besides, there were certain enviable perks attached to being a celebrity. Notably, it became *de rigueur*
for women at the Acid Tests to be balled by the fantastic
Neal Cassady. "They flew up from San Diego and drove
down from Oregon," said Ann Murphy. "It was an event,
like going to Disneyland." It was a countercultural cre-
dential, like being on Kesey's bus, or going down with
Janis.

There was an undisguised messianic purpose behind the Tests. "We're already moved out of the Age of

Pisces into the Aquarian Age," Kesey said to one interviewer about this time. "The millennium started some
months ago." Neal gladly contributed his charisma to the
cause. More, he took to drumming up converts in his
own special way. He would comb the suburbs, ride up
and down among the tract houses, looking for women
who struck him as peculiarly ripe. "I think he could look
them in the eye and instantly know they were a little bit
demented," said Mountain Girl. "He'd find out where
they lived and he'd hang around their yards for hours. Of
course he wanted to get laid, but he also wanted to turn
them on to drugs and to blow their minds." His con-
quests were innumerable, and legendary. There was, for
one, the story of how he seduced the lady psychiatrist
sent by a wealthy Atherton mother to save a deranged
daughter who had been holed up with Neal for five days
in the back of the family station wagon, of how upon
following the daughter home Neal serially seduced the
mother and the nurse hired to keep the daughter from
further degeneracy.

"Do you feel your belly writhe when you pass a
woman?" Cassady wrote to Ginsberg during the forties.
"Can you see every infinitesimal particle of their souls at
a glance? at a sick loathing glance? –fuck it." Neal had
never been known to pick his women for their skill at
arranging flowers, or even for their wit or good looks.
Carolyn excepted, he had always sought out women that
society considered strange, often psychotic. Prior to joining the Pranksters, he had come to think himself sick, to
loathe himself for his insatiable desire for what the rest

of the world regarded as "tainted meat." The Pranksters, however, venerated Neal for his democratic appetites. They saw, too, what others missed: that he took seriously hung-up women who were in many cases attractive to no one else, and released them into full sensuality and self-esteem, into what Norman Mailer would call "the time of their time." The Pranksters saw as well that Neal *learned* from his aberrant women. Finally, the merry company simply marveled at the pyrotechnics of what was called "Cassady's circus." "Neal would take his women through a whole lifetime of relationships in about an hour," said Jerry Garcia. "He would keep them up for a week and they'd all become sort of blank from the intensity of the relationship." All but one, perhaps: Ann Murphy, a pen-etrating, red-haired and, to her sorrow, small-breasted woman who in another life might have been a street poet, but in this one usually looked as though she'd just been tossed out of a bar.

She had first met Cassady briefly at the home of mutual friends in 1962. A few days later he showed up unannounced at her room, where she was in bed with hepatitis. Registering every "particle of her soul" in a single glance, he promptly unzipped his fly and unveiled what she called "his thick eight inches," so to inspire her to a quick recovery. What ensued was a knock-down, drag-out relationship between two feisty Celts that lasted five years, a desanitized version of the John Wayne-Maureen O'Hara donnybrook in *The Quiet Man*.

True to pattern, Cassady scandalized this new lover's values and upbringing. She was a free spirit, but she was not prepared to live naked in the absolute present, to be utterly dependent upon Neal's ability to hustle a place to sleep, a means of locomotion, food to eat. She was desperately in love with Neal but hopelessly monogamous, and she was forced to share him with, among other members of the "circus," a gorgeous teenage blonde called June the Goon and another girl named Sharon who wore granny glasses and Buster Brown shoes. Her life with Neal cost her almost everything: It cost her, above all, her child, Grant, whose custody she lost when she was busted for drugs.

Ann Murphy referred to Cassady as "muscles, meat, and metaphysics": She was in thrall to his mind and to the mercury of his lovemaking. One moment he was a "holy man" quoting Edgar Cayce, even during intercourse. The next he was venting his jealousy and his self-loathing for wallowing in sexuality, venting what Carolyn cited as his residual Roman Catholicism. Initially Ann felt that Neal used the fantasies of her promiscuity to spice up the sex act. Soon, however, fantasy merged with reality, and Neal was punishing her corporeally for imaginary infidelities. What is more, Ann found that she was lending herself to his fantasies and enacting the very deeds he accused her of. She discovered herself on one noteworthy occasion being "joyously gang-banged" by a parade of Hell's Angels right in front of Neal, who climbed on at the end and thereby recreated a version of his own initial sexual experience under his father's gaze with the German-American brothers and sisters in that barn outside Denver.

"Neal had a fantastic power over people," said
Mountain Girl, "and it was all benign." The point, like
most points worth making, is arguable. Neal was responsible for Mountain Girl's joining the Pranksters—he
collected her on one of his recruiting forays—but she was
never a performer in Cassady's circus. Once Neal discovered that she was from an educated East Coast family
and that her given name was *Carolyn* Adams, he marked
her off limits. Thus, Mountain Girl enjoyed his influence
without, perhaps, paying its price. Jerry Garcia said that
had there been no Neal in his life there might well have
been no band called the Grateful Dead, whose improvisa-
tory sense-drunk music was a hallmark of the era. "Until
I met Neal, I was heading toward being a graphic artist,"
said Garcia. "It wasn't as if he said, 'Jerry, my boy, the
whole ball of wax happens here and now.' It was watching him move, having my mind blown by how deep he
was, how much he could take into account in any given
moment and be really in time with it. He helped us be
the kind of band we are, a concert not a studio band. For
me, making a record is like building a ship in a bottle.
Playing live music is like being in a rowboat in the
ocean."

In the post-LSD world, the usual standards of
morality did not apply. That Neal virtually raped his
women, that he would borrow a car and total it with
little compunction, that he was perpetually hustling everyone for everything—these leaden details did not dim
his aura for the Pranksters, at least not during the early,
halcyon days of the sixties. Indeed, each of his "vices"

when perceived from a different vantage could be construed as virtue. "Cassady had his subtleties," said Paul Foster, a fellow speed freak and constant companion. "If he wanted the host of the particular house he was in to roll a joint, he would, in his continuing riff, work into it how he had gone with a friend to some *joint*. And if the word would arouse in the guy the idea, fine. If not, not. He was ethical. He taught me: You go into somebody's house, the first thing you do is look in the refrigerator. If you see it is well stocked you ask for a lid of cocaine and a ten-dollar advance. If, however, there is in the corner of the refrigerator only a wrinkled parsnip, you see what you can do for them."

Neal Cassady was, said Kesey, "irrevocably beyond category." He was someone to whom such distinctions as hip versus compulsive, moral versus immoral, were impertinent. He lived by his wits. He was a trickster like Brer Rabbit or Coyote. Yet he was Christ-like in his kindness and generosity. "He made no distinction between morons and millionaires," said Mountain Girl. "They were all valuable to him." He was not merely the "fastestmanalive," but in the comics-saturated Prankster world view, Superman himself. He was, as well—somewhat paradoxically, and more poignantly—unaccommodated man, as starkly unadorned as one of Giacometti's sculptures. "He presented a model of how far you could take yourself with the most minimal resources," said Jerry Garcia. "Neal had no tools. He didn't even have work. He had no focus, really. His focus was just himself and time."

For Ginsberg, Kerouac, Carolyn, Kesey, Garcia,
and Ann Murphy, Cassady was a force that impelled
them to radically new perceptions of their own pos-
sibilities. To differing degrees, he bullied them into culs-
de-sac where they were made to embrace the "Not-Me."
He taunted them by example, required them to stretch to
keep his outrageous company, and thereby forced them
to locate a new personal center far to the left of the mass
of civilized humanity. Fortunately, they were, at least
where Neal was concerned, resilient people. They could
support his influence. Some were not so lucky.

For Paul Foster, who became a born-again Christian after the Prankster heyday, it was, according to a
friend, "either Jesus or the sleep that rots." For another of
Cassady's close companions, a onetime Stanford tennis
star in the Jack Armstrong mold, there has as yet been no
reprieve: only, since the sixties, a vegetable like existence
in the Michigan town where he grew up. "All along the
roadside," said Wavy Gravy, "you see the smattered and
charred and twisted remains of people who had fairly
loose heads and who, in an effort to emulate Cassady,
burned themselves. I'm not talking about ten or twenty
people. I'm talking about hundreds who read *On the
Road* and were turned on by the Prankster mystique and
who wanted nothing more than to be Neal Cassady.
They'd take a lot of pills and they'd fry their brains and
that would be it.... I used to tour with this piano player
named Thelonius Monk, who said, 'You know, every man
is a genius just being his own self.' Neal was Neal, ten
things at once and nothing twice. People took it upon

themselves to follow Neal. He never sought it out. He was a pretty substantial dude."

On January 17, 1966, the court in Redwood City finally decided what to do with Kesey. It sentenced him to six months in a work camp and three years' probation. The sentence was tolerable, even amusing, since the work camp was within a hefty stone's throw of Kesey's house in La Honda. Unfortunately, the court attached a rider to its decision: Kesey would have to sell his place and take his Neon Renaissance forever out of San Mateo County.

A few days after the sentence was passed down, however, Kesey and Mountain Girl were rousted by San Francisco police atop Stewart Brand's apartment building in North Beach. In their possession was a bag containing 3.54 grams of marijuana. It was at that point that Kesey decided to head south to Mexico. He would attempt to disguise his flight with a prank: an elaborate suicide note wrought in grandiose tones under LSD, which was to be left in a panel truck in Oregon, his sky-blue boots near the edge of a precipice from which it would be inferred he had hurled himself. The Great Suicide Caper fizzled, however, when Kesey's stand-in, his look-alike cousin Dee, had to have the panel truck towed near Eureka, California, and when the Humboldt County Police judged the suicide note too mannered to be credible.

The Acid Tests continued during Kesey's absence, with Ken Babbs taking over as the leader, but by early spring much of the Prankster retinue had joined Kesey in Mexico, including Cassady and Mountain Girl, who was pregnant with Sunshine, Kesey's baby. The merry crew kept on the move, but hardly maintained a low profile in Puerto Vallarta, Mazatlán, Guadalajara, Mexico City—in fact, they continued to hold Acid Tests. An agent of Interpol spotted them at the Test in Guadalajara. But he was also simultaneously picked out by the Pranksters, whose tactic was, as ever, to subvert The Enemy by involving him in "meta-game." Surprised that he'd been recognized, the agent told them that he was in Mexico looking for a Russian spy. Great! said the merry company; we'll help you. "We played that game with him the whole time we were in Mexico," Kesey would say, "always pretending he and us were after the Roosian spy; and we never wound up in jail in Mexico. I mean, he got to know us, and we kept talking about the Russian spy, and he sampled a little bit of our thing, and he came to like us, and he told his people don't bother those guys, they're all right. We did the most outrageous things in Mexico and never got in trouble."

So passed the months south of the border. Come fall, Kesey realized that it was time to return stateside and "face the man." He had two immediate goals: to move about in the USA as a fugitive and thereby to "rub salt in the wounds of J. Edgar Hoover," and to counsel his hippie flock that it was time to take the revolution "beyond acid." He wanted them to understand that the white crystal in the gelatin capsule known as LSD was but a key to open a door. It was not The Mystery itself, and one could not keep going through the same door

over and over and expect to get anywhere, to make any
real progress toward personal divinity.

Kesey was caught by the law in October, but not
before he had made sensational surprise appearances at
the San Francisco State College "trips festival," at the first
major Haight-Ashbury "be-in" and on television with San
Francisco news personality Roger Grimsby. More and
more he saw himself as someone, like John F. Kennedy or
Jesus, who was charged with a mission to change the
world. As late as the summer of 1967, serving out his
time at the work camp near La Honda, Kesey retained
his faith in himself and the hippie movement. "The
movement is growing and will last a long time," he told
interviewer Burton H. Wolfe in *The Hippies*. "One reason
is that it's based on a life-pulsating rhythm, an upbeat
that is vibrating through the universe turning on people."
He spoke of the difference in vital "meter" between the
pre- and post-World War II generations. The old meter
had been trochaic: *life*-death, *life*-death, *life*-death; there
was a total impact, then decay. The new meter was
regeneratively iambic; death-*life*, death-*life*, death-*life*.
"These kids have a certain upbeat that makes them
unlike anyone before them except Neal Cassady," said
Kesey, "and they will be that way forever."

As it turned out, Kesey was overly optimistic
about the hippie movement. And he had been, for some
time, inattentive to the change in Cassady's "beat," which
was regressing from the iamb of death-*life* to the trochee
of *life*-death. Maybe it took a relative outsider like Robert

Stone to see, as early as the summer of 1966 in Mexico, that Neal was in bad shape, that his emotions were increasingly unreal, increasingly a function of the amphetamine he was shooting up. Convinced, perhaps, of Superman's immunity, few could have given much thought to this warning circulating in the underground press:

*Speed kills.*
*It really does.*
*Amphetamine,*
*methedrine, etc.*
*can and will rot your*
*teeth, freeze your mind*
*and kill your body. The*
*life expectancy of the average*
*speed freak from the first shot*
*to the morgue is less than five years.*
*What a drag.*

In 1967 Neal's teeth were still good—they were always good—and he was without the signal buzz of the speed freak in eclipse. It was apparent, however, that he was losing his sense of fun and that he was becoming unavailable to personal contact. At the same time, his needs and demands on those around him were rising to the point of being intolerable.

"Neal made the mistake at the end of thinking he had no friends," said Paul Foster. But he was not entirely mistaken. Bill Burroughs had once observed that Cassady seemed to feel that others were "under a mysterious obligation to support him." For several years he found that support with the Pranksters, who were happy to meet his needs until his humanity and special magic became so attenuated that he could no longer offer a return on their investment. As more than one Prankster would say, "Neal burned out compassion in his friends."

"He used to say you have to be out there on the edge all the time to know who you are. You have to take your self to the brink of disaster and keep it out there as long as you can," Mountain Girl would recall. "But he was becoming worried about getting older and fearful of death." His body was betraying him. His instincts were dulled. He was slowing down. Years earlier his Cayce mentor had warned that one day his body would simply cease to respond to chemical stimuli, and now that day was upon him.

Typically, Neal did not bow to circumstance, but determined to look more closely at this new context. Against certain odds, he decided to see what positive use could be made of slowing down. He began to make homeopathic experiments with barbiturates, a drug that had always been anathema to him. The way out, he reasoned, as always, had to be *through*.

"Think of it this way," said Wavy Gravy, who had himself seen similar straits. "You're this big airplane and you've been flying around the world. You decide to land. But how do you do it? How do you get the wheels down? Where's the runway? When you stop being ahead of time you're going to be stupid for weeks."

Cassady was stupid for months. There were, of course, periods of vivacity—as, for example, when in New York he and Wavy kidnapped the fey ukelelist Tiny Tim and took him up to the Cloisters to see the dawn, and when, en route, the odd couple Tiny and Neal broke into a wondrous Bing Crosby duet. Just prior to this indelible moment, however, Cassady had passed the evening dumbly ensconced before a WBAI radio microphone. No one had been able to rouse the famed monologuist to say anything.

Neal was sinking into a blankness vastly more severe than the one Kerouac had diagnosed fifteen years earlier, and he knew it. Sadly, he could not turn for help to Kerouac himself. He had not seen Jack since the epochal cross-country bus trip to New York three years earlier. Kerouac had joined the merry company for one evening's revel at an apartment at Madison Avenue and 90th Street. By the time Jack arrived everyone was dosed with acid, the music was blaring, the lights flickering. Repelled by the hippie ambience, Kerouac would speak to no one. He noted that an American flag was being used to cover a couch and quietly went over, folded the flag, then asked the Pranksters whether they were Communists. Now Jack was back in Lowell, deep in his own existential throes. The world was rolling out from under him: Sister Nin had died; Mémère had just had a stroke; his new wife, Stella, was hiding his shoes in a vain effort to keep him out of bars, where he daily sought annihilation.

Cassady *could* turn to Ginsberg, for Allen had been serving as paterfamilias to the Pranksters—actually, to the entire postwar generation. Allen had traveled all over the world eclectically pursuing his religio-poetic vocation: He had made fire magic with a North African witch doctor, chanted with Swami A. C. Bhaktivedanta, and shared a hot tub at Esalen Institute with a gaggle of Episcopalian ministers. He was widely regarded as a kind of "central casting of the underground," as the man in the know about politicians, bondsmen, physicians, pushers, newsmen, personalities who were solid with the Revolution, and as someone with sufficient heft to pivot such heavyweights into friendly activity. In the minds of the young, radicals and hippies alike, Ginsberg was the incarnation of the New Consciousness: A poster of him got up as Uncle Sam could be purchased at most any head shop.

In the spring of 1967 Cassady had broken epistolary silence to write Ginsberg two desperate notes from San Miguel de Allende, Mexico. Within lines in one note he claims first to have "big plans" and then asks Allen to "save" him: "I'm counting on you al...." Ginsberg would see Cassady several times during 1967; indeed, he was a frequent passenger on Kesey's bus. On one trip in particular, coming back from Bellingham, Washington, he and Neal would spend the night together with one of Neal's women in a San Francisco motel. "His skin was cold, chill, sweaty & corpselike," Allen would recall. "I think it was the first time I ever got out of bed with Neal voluntarily...."

Neal sensed end game, and he apparently made an effort to check in with old friends without telling them, of course, what business he was about. Notably, he drove to Denver to see the friends of his youth, Justin

Brierly, Ed White, et al. His reception was tepid at best. "I came home and he was upstairs taking a shower in one of the bathrooms," Ed White would say in an interview in the Denver *Post*. "I kind of panicked. I didn't know if he was planning to move in for a while or what. But when he came down all dressed, I gave him a beer, and I think we told him we were going out or something or else we were. I was as bad as Brierly.

"Neal had an old beat-up Pontiac station wagon or something. It was full of, it looked like sea bags. It was sort of laundry up and down. And he had on one red boot and one tan shoe, I think ... He was very kind, very nice that time. He talked about all these years that had passed. He told me I was a myth or something, and he told me he was a myth."

Neal had always been amused by the notion of being a "myth." Naturally, he had traded on it to seduce women, but he had never taken it seriously. Now finally, it was much on his mind. In a rap recorded in November 1967 by The Grateful Dead at the Straight Theater in San Francisco, Neal refers to himself as "Keroassady," a creature as much of Kerouac's confection as his own. During the rap, which was conducted with The Dead tuning up in the background, he makes numerous allusions to Kerouac and Ginsberg, to their storied doings, and even to Kesey's fugitive tête-à-tête with TV personality Roger Grimsby. The recorded hipalogue is as veined with subtle treasure as any previous effort, but it is oddly self-conscious. Neal appears to be sampling himself as a figure in history, to be at once burdened and consoled by

his enshrinement in the pantheon of American heroes.
He is also, and above all, giving the public what he
thinks it wants—even *demands*—of him.

Shortly after the stint with The Grateful Dead, he
called Carolyn from Larkspur, California. He wanted her
to please come and get him. He was sick. He said he had
been up at Kesey's new place in Oregon, where an event
was ongoing. His nerves were blitzed and everyone, he
felt, kept staring at him. They expected him to perform,
he said—expected him to be Superman, and he couldn't.
He had bolted out the door *sans* jacket and cigarettes
and had hitchhiked down the coast to a friend's.

Carolyn called old reliable Al Hinkle, and the two
of them went to retrieve Neal. It was not the first time
she had heard from Neal since the divorce. Indeed, she
would say that she and the kids probably saw more of
him after the decree than before. He never really stopped
thinking of Los Gatos as his home.

On the way back to Los Gatos, Al suggested that
Neal might be able to get his old job back. The railroad
was in dire need of experienced brakemen, and there
were new people running things who knew nothing of
Dean Moriarty, Johnny Potseed, or Speed Limit. It was
agreed that the next morning another brakeman would
take Neal to the depot and steer him to the man in
charge. Cassady seemed relieved, steadied by the prospect
of regular work.

Shortly after Al left, Carolyn looked up to find
Neal glaring down at her, a terrified quality in his eye.
"Where's John? *Where* is John!" he wanted to know. She

answered that he was visiting a friend. But Neal was already racing down the hall to John's bedroom, where he threw himself on his knees, clutched his head, and sobbed, "Oh, my *God*, I've killed my son! I've *killed* my son!" Instantly, a "past life" *tableau* of John being slashed by the knife blades of chariot wheels hung luridly in the air.

Fortunately, John soon returned to the house and Neal regained his equanimity. Later in the evening, however, Carolyn heard Neal in the bathroom over the drone of the shower pounding on the walls and shouting: He was carrying on a heated conversation with the devil, who was, he said, a constant friend/antagonist. When Neal passed out that night, numbing Carolyn's cradling arm, he slept without visible sign of breathing.

The next morning Carolyn woke him at six. He was alert, pleasant, enthusiastic, and he promised as he went out the door to be back that evening wearing the mantle of the brakeman. Two weeks later John and Jami and Jami's friend Kym ran into Neal and the Pranksters near Golden Gate Park. Neal had not been able to apply to the Southern Pacific for his old job. He had been picked up by the police, who had been hounding him, as they had throughout his life, and he had spent the fortnight in jail because of traffic warrants. Worse, he failed to recognize Jami that day in San Francisco and saddened her for his sake by repeatedly addressing her friend Kym by her name.

Some weeks later, on February 2, 1968, Neal took

a train back down to Mexico—to Celaya, from where he
caught a taxi to San Miguel de Allende. He had arranged
to stay with a twenty-two-year-old lover and disciple
named J. B. At about noon on February 3, Neal left J. B.'s
house, saying that he was returning to Celaya to pick up
appurtenances left at the depot, notably his "magic bag,"
which generally contained a Bible and items that recalled
his loved ones, maybe old letters from Ginsberg or
Kerouac. He told J. B. that he would walk the two and a
half miles to the San Miguel train station, then would
continue on to Celaya, counting the railroad ties between
the two towns. J. B. did not take this last statement
seriously, since Celaya was over fifteen miles away and
Neal's feet had been hurting him.

Arriving midafternoon at the San Miguel station,
Neal got caught up in a Mexican wedding party, at which
he apparently consumed a quantity of a muddy alcoholic
drink called *pulque* and a handful of Seconals. Primed
with "cankers and lush," the tandem that would kill
Joplin and Hendrix, Cassady was ready for one last
gratuitous "transaction" with the cosmos. He would attempt to make good on what struck J. B. as his fanciful
project of counting the ties between San Miguel and
Celaya.

The next morning a group of Indians found him
lying beside the track a mile and a half outside San
Miguel. He was comatose and would die later that
morning in a nearby hospital. The death certificate cited
"generalized congestion," but the newspapers would use

more resonant language. Cassady died of overexposure, they said. He was cremated and the ashes were entrusted to Carolyn, with whom they remain to this day.

The apocrypha that has accreted around Neal Cassady tells us that his last words were, "64,928." Legend has it that Cassady was counting the ties, that he was faithful to his part of the Promethean transaction, right up to the end.

# Afterword

This book is in large part a story of Neal Cassady's impact on the people who mattered to him. It could not have taken its particular shape without the cooperation of Mountain Girl, Wavy Gravy, Jerry Garcia, Paul Foster, Janice "J. B." Brown, Ann Murphy, Gordon Lish, Robert Stone. I am grateful to them for taking the time to talk to me. Above all, I am indebted to Carolyn Cassady, who wrote me fifteen page letters about her life with Neal, and who looked upon my project virtually as her own.

There have been some substantial things written about the Beats and their progeny. I have been ballasted by the writings of John Clellon Holmes, Seymour Krim, John Tytell, Ann Charters, Dennis McNally, Jane Kramer, Barry Gifford and Lawrence Lee, Tom Wolfe, and Carolyn Cassady. Messrs. Holmes, Krim, and Tytell were kind enough to read my manuscript—and, in several cases, to correct errors of fact and help sharpen emphases. I have, of course, drawn heavily upon the writings of Ginsberg, Kerouac, and Kesey.

I wish to thank Ken Emerson at the *New York Times Sunday Magazine* for whetting my interest in the Beats, and Dennis Fawcett, my editor at Prentice-Hall, for proposing this book. Thea Wieseltier helped with the photographs. Tom Noel verified my Denver details. Cathie Scitovsky gave me shelter in San Francisco. Gail Hochman, my agent, guided me through the dark wood of publishing and was smart about my manuscript. Also thoughtful and supportive in various ways were Reid Boates, Tom Moloney, Richard Poirier, and my parents, Bill and Gerry Plummer.

It remains to try to express my debt to Molly McKaughan, my wife. I can only say that this book was enabled by her love.

# INDEX

161